HIGHER
HIGHER EDUCATION

INTEGRATING HOLINESS INTO ALL OF CAMPUS LIFE

JONATHAN S. RAYMOND

ALDERSGATE PRESS

HIGHER HIGHER EDUCATION
By Jonathan S. Raymond

Copyright © 2015 Jonathan S. Raymond

All rights reserved. No part of this book may be reproduced, or stored in a retrieval system or transmitted in any form or by any means, electronic, mechanical, photocopying, recording, scanning or otherwise, except as permitted by the 1976 United States Copyright Act, or with the prior written permission of Aldersgate Press. Requests for permission should be addressed to the editor of Aldersgate Press, *Editor@AldersgatePress.com*.

Unless otherwise noted, all scripture quotations are from the New Revised Standard Version Bible, copyright © 1989 the Division of Christian Education of the National Council of the Churches of Christ in the United States of America. Used by permission. All rights reserved.

THE PUBLICATIONS ARM OF

HolinessandUnity.org

In Collaboration with

LAMP POST inc.
www.lamppostpublishers.com
Spring Valley, CA

Printed in the United States of America

Soft Cover ISBN 13:   978-1-60039-304-4
ebook ISBN-13:   978-1-60039-977-0

Library of Congress Control Number: 2015932898

ACKNOWLEDGEMENTS

Friends and colleagues within my own faith walk influenced the thinking that this book represents, especially Roger Green, William Francis, Michael Peterson, David Rightmire, Yvonne Moulton, Howard Snyder, Paul Rader, Steve Seamands, Lyell Rader, and Donald Burke. Those authors from whom I also have gained insight, wisdom, and inspiration become apparent throughout the book. More than anything, the occasion and initiative for writing this book came from the Wesleyan-Holiness Consortium, launched in recent years by Kevin Mannoia and others.

It was the encouragement of Barry Callen and Don Thorsen that caused me to submit a proposal for this book to the Aldersgate Press, the publishing arm of the Consortium. To these friends and colleagues I remain indebted. I am also indebted to friends of whom I know only through their writings: John Wesley, Samuel Logan Brengle, Frederick Coutts, Diane Leclerc, E. Stanley Jones, and Kenneth Collins, Richard Knight, Theodore Runyon, and so many others. Without their influence this book would not have been conceived and developed.

Finally, my wife, Irene, has always been behind the scenes with support and encouragement in all my endeavors. She is the answer to my prayers in college for a wife who is godly, lovely, and a true partner in life. At every turn in the road, she is there to cheer me on.

DEDICATION

This book is dedicated to Dr. Alan Moulton, my dear friend and esteemed mentor, who opened doors of academic opportunity and was a model of holiness in higher education. I am one of many thousands of students influenced by Dr. Moulton's faithfulness in his calling to Christian higher education in the Wesleyan-Holiness tradition.

TABLE OF CONTENTS

Acknowledgements · *iii*
Dedication · *v*

Part One · **1**
  1. Holiness and Higher Education · 3
  2. A Brief History of Christian Higher Education · · · · · · · · · · · 13
         A brief history continued . . .
  3. Not All Christians Think Alike · 31
  4. The Remnant in the Wesleyan-Holiness Context · · · · · · · · · 41

Part TWO · **47**
  5. A Heritage of Holiness · 49
  6. Reclaiming the Heritage · 61
  7. Holiness and the University · 73
  8. Holiness in the University: · 83
         Essence, Form, and Impact

PART THREE · **95**
  9. Pursuing Holiness in Higher Education · · · · · · · · · · · · · · · · 97
  10. Paradigms of Engagement · 109
  11. Serious Essentials · 125
  12. The Highest Spiritual Ends · 135

    ENDNOTES · *141*

PART ONE

CHAPTER ONE

HOLINESS AND HIGHER EDUCATION

I will utter things, things from old. We will not hide them from their children; we will tell the next generation . . .

Psalm 78:2 & 4

This book is about Christian higher education with two questions in mind: First, is there a pinnacle of higher education not yet reached and what does it look like? Second, what are the highest possible heights of Christian higher education yet to be reached? Christian higher education has been through three cycles of ascendency and decline. We now are in a fourth cycle that reflects a remarkable ascent that occasions these two questions.

After forty years working in higher education, sixteen in large public universities (full professor, tenure, etc.) and twenty-four in smaller Christian colleges and universities (Dean, Vice President, Provost, President and Vice

Chancellor), I now bring into view some realities that occasion needed conversation in answering these two questions. Hopefully, this book begins a conversation among college and university trustees, presidents, vice presidents, deans, department chairs, faculty, and student leaders. It will likely be of interest to parents considering where to send their children to school and to pastors who wish to promote venues of Christian higher education that they know and trust.

In the international rankings of universities and colleges, there are 6,000 institutions listed. More exist worldwide, but one can imagine that the list had to be cut off at some point. It is not surprising that higher education, including Christian higher education, reflects a diverse array of missions, of philosophical and theological frameworks, and methodologies for delivering education.[1] This is the case today with Christian institutions of higher learning, all of which differ in their historical journeys, identities, strategies, and approaches to educational vitality on their campuses.

Overview of the Book

This book is about the appropriate relationship of holiness and higher learning. It is divided into three parts and thirteen chapters. In part one, the introduction shares my personal journey. I am a product of a Wesleyan-Holiness home, denomination, and college. In a personal way, I hope to contextualize subsequent insights into the topic of holiness and higher education.

The first four chapters discuss four waves that make up the historical and contemporary contexts of Christian higher education. A specific focus in chapter three is on institutions of higher learning in a Wesleyan-Holiness tradition. In chapter four, both fidelity to and drift from the moorings of historical Wesleyan-Holiness institutions of higher education is discussed. Many Wesleyan-Holiness colleges took the path of intentional disengagement from the church, initially an unintentional drift from faith so characteristic of higher education broadly. For a remnant of a relatively few, the path was one of fidelity to their Wesleyan roots and even the renewal of Wesleyan-Holiness priorities. This is discussed in chapter five.

Part two presents the way forward. It makes the case that the fidelity to holiness by the remnant of Wesleyan-Holiness institutions is key to reclaiming their heritage and furthering John Wesley's vision of spreading scriptural holiness throughout the land. Chapter six discusses the prospect of universities and colleges promoting a deeper appreciation for and embrace of the essence of holiness and its origins and implications for development of the whole person. Chapter seven offers a discussion of the recent initiatives of the Wesleyan-Holiness Consortium in reclaiming a holiness heritage for today's churches and campuses. Chapter eight poses the idea that ultimate educational vitality is holiness at the heart of the university and may be pursued as an ultimate student outcome. Chapter nine presents the way forward in the pursuit of holiness at the center of the higher education enterprise.

> My five years as a doctoral student was a period of neglect. I neglected spiritual disciplines, or what John Wesley called "means of grace," the very means by which we grow in our faith and relationship with Christ. I neglected to read my Bible, pray, worship, enjoy Christian fellowship, attend church, and participate within a faith community. At best, I was a minimalist when it came to practicing my faith.

Part three covers the serious pursuit of Wesleyan-Holiness in higher education as the ultimate spiritual outcome in a higher form of higher education. Chapter ten sheds light on holiness as a new pinnacle for higher education in student outcomes and faculty scholarship. Chapter eleven presents four paradigms of engagement that frame the holistic approach to higher education by the whole university or college for the whole person. Chapter twelve discusses the serious organizational essentials necessary for successful engagement in Wesleyan-Holiness higher education. Finally, chapter thirteen addresses the Wesleyan-Holiness orientation to university and college education as the way to achieving the highest spiritual ends of holiness and God's equipping graduates to do immeasurably more than they could ask or imagine for the Kingdom of God.

This book speaks first to a readership within the Wesleyan-Holiness tradition and sphere of influence. It is also written to engage discussion with other faith communities who are synergistic in their soteriology and pneumatology. Finally, it is written for those looking to take higher learning to higher heights of fidelity to our shared biblical call in Christian higher education. It is my abiding hope that we will together discover a higher Christian higher education to the glory of God and the advancement of God's kingdom.

Discovering a Higher Higher Education

In many ways this book emerges out of my own personal experience in a tradition of Wesleyan holiness and forty years of teaching as a doctoral student and professor within public universities for sixteen years, and working as a chief academic officer and president within private (Christian) institutions of higher learning for twenty-four years. Throughout a life of being, doing, and achieving, I now have particular insights and settled views regarding a higher form of higher education. Life does that. It crafts our views and shapes our insights. In this sense, this book shares reflections occasioned by my personal journey both outside and within Christian higher education.

My life in higher education started as a first-year student in 1966. For four years as an undergraduate at Asbury College and five years at the University of Kentucky, I was on the receiving end as a student. Thanks to the blessed mentoring of my major professor, Dr. Alan Moulton, I graduated in 1970 and went directly into a doctoral program at the University of Kentucky. The years 1970 to 1990 included an immersion into the social-political-spiritual ecologies of large public universities (U. of Kentucky, U. of Maryland, Arizona State U., and the U. of Hawaii). This twenty-year trek through public universities occasioned a significant dissipation of my faith, a rediscovery of my personal relationship with Christ, a gradual growth in grace, and finally a maturity of faith and Christian living.

> My depression and paralyzed psyche were in direct conflict with my head and heart. It was in that dark place of depression, with the help of a little book, that the light and love of God was shed generously in my heart and mind.

When I have the opportunity to share my story about the spiritual dissipation of my faith, it sometimes surprises people. My five years as a doctoral student was a period of neglect. I neglected spiritual disciplines, or what John Wesley called "means of grace," the very means by which we grow in our faith and relationship with Christ. I neglected to read my Bible, pray, worship, enjoy Christian fellowship, attend church, and participate within a faith community. At best, I was a minimalist when it came to practicing my faith. My failing faith walk with Christ created a vacuum.

To exacerbate the situation, for five consecutive research projects, the last one being my dissertation, I investigated what social psychologists call "moral attributions." This field of inquiry plunged me into moral behavior theory, moral philosophy, and ethics. Later I realized that I was steadily working my way into a spiritual-emotional crisis. Where there is a vacuum, something will fill it. My minimalist approach to faith was not progressing forward. Rather I was losing ground. My spiritual vitality and joy were dissipating while my intellect about moral principles, moral reasoning, and moral/ethical theory was expanding. Faith will dissipate when not exercised. There is no such thing as a static position when it comes to matters of faith. The result of my spiritual decline was serious.

By the fall of 1974, I was ready to write the doctoral dissertation. Since I had abandoned my Christian commitments and way of life, I had seven days a week to write. Teaching two classes at the University of Kentucky and one class at Transylvania University in Lexington, however, did not provide enough time and leave enough energy to do the writing. Irene and I took up residence in a little one-bedroom house in the piney woods of south Georgia. While she taught junior high English and Spanish, I worked at home trying to get some traction on the dissertation. Irene's father was a Methodist pastor in a little church not more than a hundred yards from our front door, so we began attending church again. Then the crisis hit. I was in a full-blown depression. I was lost between my upbringing in a very nurturing Christian home and family where I was highly discipled and my five years of faith neglect and dissipation. My head and heart were raised to love the Lord with all my heart, mind, and soul, and to trust in the person of Jesus Christ. My head was disengaged from my heart.

By the time I was writing the dissertation and trying to finish the doctorate, my heart was cold. The person of Jesus was a distant memory. I intellectually embraced the belief that Christian principles did not differ from other universal expressions of principles in Marxism, socialism, Buddhism, Islam, and other faiths and philosophies. This is a common result of the dissipation of faith. The belief in Christian principles remained. I had a broad grasp of universal moral principles, but the belief in the universal Christ was lost. Acceptance of Christ as a person lessened. The presence of Christ in my life became unfamiliar, unrecognized, and unacknowledged. Christ had not abandoned me. I had drifted into abandonment of Him. I became distracted from continuing my personal, active relationship to Him. A Christ-shaped vacuum developed in my life. Vacuums will always be filled by something.

The intellectual content of my studies filled my vacuum. This was so dissonant. It was in direct conflict with all I had grown to know and love spiritually in the past. Up until my doctoral studies, I had experienced a higher form of education, one that integrated the head and the heart with the idea of holiness. As an undergraduate, this guided my life. Five years later, as I struggled to complete the dissertation, I realized that I had lost my way. My depression and paralyzed psyche were in direct conflict with my head and heart. It was in that dark place of depression, with the help of a little book, that the light and love of God was shed generously in my heart and mind.

Five years before, at the time of graduation from Asbury College, I had purchased a little book of devotions written by E. Stanley Jones, *The Word Became Flesh*. For five years of doctoral studies, it just sat on the bookshelf ignored. Since writing the dissertation had ground to a halt, I decided to read. I spotted the Jones book, picked it up, and began. I read all 365 devotionals. By the end of the day, Jones had reintroduced me to the person of Jesus Christ. The book was filled with scripture and wisdom. It was a massive exposure to God's means of grace. It filled my vacuum, reminding me page after page that we must go beyond universal principles in our efforts to find truth and live life fully.

Intellectually, I found non-Christians preferred to discuss Christian principles rather than the Person of Christ. From E. Stanley Jones I began to see that principles invite study, weighing and debate. The Person of Jesus demands decision and commitment. Principles only ask for mental ascent, but the Person of Jesus demands dedication. The world is always ready to embrace universal principles, but we are called to follow the incarnate Christ. Principles say, "Ponder this." Christ says, "Follow me." Principles are the word become word, philosophy. Christ in us is the Word become flesh.

While throughout my doctoral studies I embraced discussions of ethics and universal principles, Jones's little book was a refreshing reminder and help to embrace Jesus Christ, the only truly worthy object of my faith. In short, with Jones's help, my depression lifted. I hit the restart button of faith and finished the dissertation within two months. I picked up my journey with Christ again. Ever since, I have experienced a holiness journey with over forty years of exposure to God's grace and encounters with

Christ the Person through the Holy Spirit, and forty years of serving in higher education. Along the way I have discovered a *higher* higher education that makes possible the ultimate student outcome, being filled to the fullness of God in Christ-likeness and holiness.

I write out of my personal experience and faith journey. With settled views, this discussion is grounded in an appreciation of holiness, both personal and social, as the highest aspiration of Christian life and life in Christian community. An understanding of the essence of holiness occasions a view of the history of Christian higher education, the heritage of holiness within Christian higher education, and suggests a way forward in pursuing a higher goal for higher learning.

By way of introduction, two realities strike me as paralleling personal wholeness and well- being. One is that it is possible to personally drift away from centeredness in Christ. Such drift is fostered by other attractions and distractions, often in a particular social context. Faith and commitment to Christ can dissipate merely through benign neglect. Consequently, a vacuum takes place and other priorities fill the void.

What is possible at a personal level may also occur at an institutional level. Christian colleges and universities can drift and decline. Their Christ-centered priorities can shift. Their centeredness in Christ can slowly change for the worse. This explains the history of Christian higher education over the past four centuries. Secondly, it is possible to avoid the drift and dissolution of faith and commitment. And it is possible to rediscover and reclaim one's first love, first mission, and first commitment. Both person and institution can find the way back. It is possible to go on to new heights of a *higher* higher education.

Finally, at the heart of this discussion is John Wesley's theology of spiritual formation in the context of the Kingdom of God. Why Wesley? Wesley brings clarity and balance to classic Christian orthodoxy. He was a don at Oxford where he taught Greek. He had his students read and discuss with him the writings of the early church fathers, the Patristics:

Clement of Rome, Justin Martyr, Irenaeus, Gregory of Nyssa, Vincent of Lerius, Cyril of Alexandria, and others. His immersion in the apostolic and patristic writings, discussions, and records of the early councils and synods shaped his "conjunctive" theology of salvation from the darkest of sin to the restoring light of holiness and Christ-likeness. His grasp of Spirit-filled, classic Christian thought makes possible a foundation of orthodoxy on which we can build a **higher** higher learning redirected toward the highest spiritual ends.

CHAPTER TWO

A BRIEF HISTORY OF CHRISTIAN HIGHER EDUCATION

> Behold, I will do a new thing, now it shall spring forth.
> *Isaiah 43:19*

At some point, I came to see that holiness could and should be at the heart of higher education. After all, wouldn't holiness be the very thing that made it even higher? It seemed reasonable that holiness would be the focal point of the mission of Christ-centered, Christian higher education. Spiritual formation and maturity would serve the ultimate end of personal and social holiness.

Alas! In the domain of higher education, holiness is not taught, nor is it considered to be even a viable (in some cases achievable) student outcome. If it were, it would occasion very different thinking about the ultimate goals of higher education. It would impact how we think about curriculum and the milieu of a Christian university or college. Holiness would be viewed as the pinnacle of human development, worthy of scholarship, investigation, and discussion regarding its social, political, and spiritual implications for students. There is no record that this has ever been the case.

Over nearly 1500 years at least four historic waves of Christian faith-based higher education can be identified. In all four waves, holiness has not been an explicit interest. This is true in the creation and dissemination of knowledge by colleges and universities broadly and even in those grounded in the Christian faith. The noble intent of many for centuries has been to develop godly Christian graduates of competence and character, at first for church service, but then also to impact the various marketplaces of life. However noble the intentions, there is a long history of missional drift and a dissipation of faith away from the initial essence, mission, and intentional ends of Christian higher education.

In the more recent public sector, the aspirations for success are quite narrow and prescribed. One colleague at a national gathering of university presidents was heard to say, "The purpose of universities is to produce and disseminate knowledge. Period." This was an expression of the normative dogma of public universities. The declaration brought an enthusiastic response from the room full of university presidents who strongly agreed. At the time, I thought it was an overly simplistic vision of the potential of higher education. It was naïve and small-minded.

I knew the particular president who said this. I knew that he had an active, personal faith, but was not inclined to bring the spheres of faith and life in Christ together through a president's leadership of the university. If pressed, I am sure that most colleague presidents in that room would agree that another central aspiration of all universities is to produce graduates of competence at all levels, but especially at the doctoral level, graduates who would go on to fame and fortune as alumni.

A BRIEF HISTORY OF CHRISTIAN HIGHER EDUCATION

Knowledge and money and influence were (are) the twin and often only goals of higher education.

Christian higher education ideally aspires to more. The hope in the private, Christian sector is that graduates will go out into the world and address the world's needs for leadership in both competence and character. The missing element in leadership too often is character. By character we mean competence in a chosen field and character after the likeness of Jesus Christ.

From a Wesleyan-Holiness point of view, Christ-like character is holiness, the personal presence of Christ in the human heart and the social-spiritual presence of Christ in the faith community. It is the provision of God's holy love by divine grace empowering us to love the Lord with all our heart, mind, soul and strength and our neighbor as ourselves. With all our heart implies the life of heart holiness. With all our mind implies an integration of faith and reason with heart holiness. It is a love that is grasped with an understanding that surpasses knowledge (Ephesians 3:18), knowledge of the head *and* the heart.

> Over nearly 1500 years at least four historic waves of Christian faith-based higher education can be identified. In all four waves, holiness has not been an explicit interest. This is true in the creation and dissemination of knowledge by colleges and universities broadly and even in those grounded in the Christian faith.

First Wave: The Christian Roots of Higher Education

The enterprise of higher education antedates the Greeks in Mesopotamia and Egypt, including the establishment of libraries in support of teaching. The liberal arts tradition in the Western world dates back as early as three centuries before Christ with the *quadrivium* (arithmetic, geometry, astronomy, and music) and the *trivium* (grammar, logic, and geometry). Such education was intended to produce a civilized citizenry for society.[2]

Over the next several hundred years, many ancient academic centers of learning flourished until the Emperor, Justinian, closed the Athens School of Wisdom in 529 A.D. Such schools were proscribed and abandoned along with the idea of the liberal arts. Subsequently, monasteries became involved with academies. Within monasteries, *Scriptoria* (copy houses) were established to reproduce the scriptures and other writings, both holy and secular. Over time, monastic and cathedral schools were established. Monastic schools served the monk population. Cathedral schools offered general studies and served clergy and the wealthy laity. Within this Christian context over the centuries, higher education took the form of the Christian liberal arts and became the building blocks of universities by the twelfth century. We see this in the founding of universities at Bologna (1088), Salamanca (1130), and Paris (1200).

In the cathedral schools, the general studies, *studium generales*, set the pattern for higher education. In the beginning of Oxford (1096 teaching began; the actual founding date is unknown) a student would enroll in a college of general studies, not a college of professional studies. Higher education, and in particular the liberal arts, survived in Christian form. The word university was coined by the University of Bologna and roughly meant "community of teachers and scholars" (*universitas magistrorum et scholarium*). It is said that higher education in the Western world is not the heir and successor of Athens or Alexandria, but of Paris, Bologna, Oxford, and the Christian college model that they established. This was the first wave of Christian higher education.

Second Wave: The Colonial Colleges

Like the Latin American colonial universities of the sixteenth century, the Christian university model was appropriated from Europe and England and transplanted to North American soil. This first took place in the establishment of Harvard College (allegedly in 1636 by John Harvard).[3] While the Pilgrims founded Plymouth in 1620 for religious reasons, the Puritans founded Salem in 1623 and the village of Boston in 1630, both for business purposes. Boston soon became the political, commercial, financial, religious, and educational center of New England.

Founded "for Christ and the Church," Harvard College provided the dominant model for the colonial establishment of Christian higher education in North America for the next two hundred years. Harvard framed the model for other church-based institutions, including the College of William and Mary (1693), Yale (1701), Princeton (1746), the University of Pennsylvania (1751), Columbia (1754), Brown (1764), and Dartmouth (1769). The array of colonial colleges established in the New World of North America were all founded by Christians, including Harvard (Puritans), College of William and Mary (by Royal Charter and hence Anglican as a "perpetual college of divinity, philosophy, languages, and the good arts and sciences"), Yale (Puritans), Princeton (Presbyterians), Pennsylvania (Quakers), Columbia (Anglicans), Brown (Baptist and Congregational), and Dartmouth (Congregational).

The colonial colleges before the American Revolution represent a first wave of Christian higher education in North America. Theologically speaking, it was a wave of Calvinism. The colonial colleges had in common the Reformed, Calvinist roots of their founders (mostly Puritans, Congregationalists, and Presbyterians). They also had in common the development of Christian higher education in the spiritual and cultural context of what became known as the First Great Awakening.

The First Great Awakening revitalized Christian (Protestant) Europe and the American colonies for two decades (1730s and 1740s), but the impact on religious life lasted far longer. In part, this was through the influence of the faith-based colonial colleges where clergy leadership was trained and shaped for life-long ministry. It began with the preaching of Jonathan Edwards in New England and was augmented by the Reformed preaching of evangelist George Whitfield, a close friend of John and Charles Wesley.

HIGHER HIGHER EDUCATION

The First Great Awakening occasioned strong preaching for decades to follow. It promoted a deep conviction in the congregations of a personal need for salvation. The Christian faith was made deeply personal. The necessity of a personal response to one's conviction of sin, the need for redemption, and an emotional commitment to Christ became the explicit standard of personal morality. The First Great Awakening primarily impacted Reformed Protestant congregations in the Northeast colonies, affecting persons who were already church members—Congregational, Presbyterian, Dutch Reformed, and German Reformed churches with some impact on Baptist and Methodist congregations as well.

> Religion had little impact on the lives of the people. Churches were subsidized by the government. Pastors, paid from taxes, never set foot in their parishes (appointments). With the exception of dissenters like the Puritans, every bit of enthusiasm for faith was gone in the nation. Spiritual vitality was not to be found. English religion was as dry as dust.

The emphasis of the First Great Awakening was not so much on holiness, but rather on initial salvation, justification by grace through faith. Its roots were solidly in Calvinism and largely expressed evangelical Calvinism. While it brought a great increase in the number of believers who experienced salvation, it also proved to be divisive between old-school Calvinists who wished to protect the importance of doctrine and ritual and new-school, early American revivalists who favored emotional expressions of faith and revivals with outpourings of the Holy Spirit.[4]

The colonial colleges of the impacted denominations were awakened as well. Their commitment to their missions was renewed for a time, but personal and institutional commitments to their founding missions gradually dissipated along with faith. By the Second Great Awakening, the colleges founded in the colonial period had drifted in their faith commitments to embrace deism, Unitarian universalism, and eventually generic moral philosophy apart from Christian faith. The loss of Christian faith and a

Christ-centered worldview characterized all of the colonial colleges by the mid-nineteenth century as the Second Great Awakening was getting underway and proliferating new Christian colleges and universities across the nation.

Another Kind of Great Awakening

While the First Great Awakening was unfolding in the colonies, another kind of great awakening was taking place in England. Faith and religion were in a deplorable state of decay and the British economy was in a massive shift from agriculture to industry. This shift occasioned a tsunami of change in the culture. In the words of Charles Dickens, "It was the best of times and the worst of times." The best of times came to business people who owned mills and factories. They realized an economic boom and a time of great luxury at the pinnacle of the expansion of the British Empire.

If you were not in business, it was the worst of times. Most people were desperately poor, impoverished workers living in misery. In France, just across the channel from England, the revolution evoked a violent upheaval. In England, the revolution was quiet, orderly, and spiritual. In France, change came by armed revolutionaries. In England, the Anglican revivalists John and Charles Wesley and their lay assistants led a Wesleyan-Holiness revolution that spiritually engaged a significant portion of the population.

The church at the time was in a sad state of deterioration and decay. The Church of England served the upper classes. For decades it drifted into superficial worldliness, deism, and a lifestyle of indulgence. Religion had little impact on the lives of the people. Churches were subsidized by the government. Pastors, paid from taxes, never set foot in their parishes (appointments). With the exception of dissenters like the Puritans, every bit of enthusiasm for faith was gone in the nation. Spiritual vitality was not to be found. English religion was as dry as dust.

It was in this sad context that John Wesley started a revival that was spiritually revolutionary. His aim was to reform the Church of England. His preaching of holiness and his organization of Methodist Societies across England, and eventually the British Empire, was transformational far beyond the Church of England. His calling and initiative was to "spread scriptural holiness across the land." The progress of the Wesleyan movement across England, Ireland, and Scotland reached the new United States and Canada at a time between the First and Second Great Awakenings. There it set the stage for a different kind of great awakening and the remarkable rise and expansion of Christian higher education in America.

CHAPTER THREE

THE RISE AND FALL OF CHRISTIAN HIGHER EDUCATION:

A brief history continued . . .

> Those who abide in me [Jesus] and I in them bear much fruit.... Whoever does not abide in me is thrown away like a branch and withers.
>
> *John 15:5-6*

Over a period of 160 years (1790–1950), the new United States witnessed a remarkable rise and fall of Christian higher education. As the nation's expansive westward movement unfolded, new towns and cities sprang up with all the infrastructure one might expect, including churches and institutions of higher learning begun by churches. This growth in the founding of colleges and universities across the nation was the third wave in the history of Christian higher education. For a multitude of reasons, as the culture of the nation changed, so did the nature of higher education institutions, including an estrangement of faith and learning, the rift between church and academy, and the separation of personal piety from the quest for academic excellence.

Third Wave: Colleges of the New Nation

Colleges of the new United States comprised the Third Wave of Christian higher education in America. Their advent brought into being a small tsunami of hundreds of new colleges and universities. Once they began to mature, they failed to hold on to the distinctives of their Christian character. The reasons are understandable.

Seventy to eighty years after its beginning, the First Great Awakening was subsiding among Reformed congregations. A Second Great Awakening began in the relatively new United States. While the First Great Awakening took place largely among those who were churched in Reformed congregations, the second was an outreach movement to the unchurched. While the Reformed congregations settled down in the larger cities and states on the east coast of the new country, others—including Wesley's Methodists and the Baptists—moved west as the population continued to push the edge of the frontier further toward the Pacific. As the nation grew, Methodists sent circuit-riding lay preachers out into the frontier. New villages and towns sprang up. Churches and eventually Christian colleges were started. The Second Great Awakening occasioned a tremendous rise in the number of local churches across the new nation.

The Second Great Awakening occurred in episodic revivals (1790-1840; 1850–1900) and across several denominations. The nature of the revivals reflected the theology of each denomination. Out of the revival awakening, church membership rose dramatically among all denominations, especially among Baptists and Methodists. Baptists moved in and evangelized the Tidewater South and established a strong presence in the towns and cities proliferating west and south of the Allegheny Mountains and far beyond. Millions of new members came into existing evangelical denominations. The Methodists gained more than other denominations as their itinerant preachers and circuit riders moved westward with the expanding nation. They accounted for more than half of all church members by 1840.

As new towns and churches were built, the Methodists founded institutions of higher learning, schools, institutes, colleges and universities. The Methodist list is long. It includes Allegheny College (1815), McKendree University (1828), LaGrange College (1831), Emory University (1836), Duke University (1838), DePauw University (1837), Boston University (1839), Wesleyan College (1839), Ohio Wesleyan University (1842), Willamette University (1842), Baldwin Wallace University (1845), Otterbein University (1847), Illinois Wesleyan University (1850), University of the Pacific (formerly California Wesleyan University, 1851), Hamline University (1854), Tennessee Wesleyan University (1857), Kentucky Wesleyan University (1858), University of Denver (1864), Drew University (1867), Syracuse University (1870), The University of Southern California (1880), Florida Southern University (1883), Kansas Wesleyan (1886), Texas Wesleyan University (1890), West Virginia Wesleyan College (1890), and some one hundred other colleges and universities affiliated with the United Methodist Church today. Wheaton College was founded by Methodists in 1860 and soon after became independent and multi-denominational.

Other institutions in the broad Wesleyan-Holiness tradition can be added to the long list of those founded in the second half of the nineteenth and early twentieth centuries: Roberts Wesleyan College (1866), Spring Arbor University (1873), Houghton College (1883), Asbury University (1890), Seattle Pacific University (1891), Greenville College (1892), Southern Wesleyan University (1906), Anderson University (1917), and Indiana Wesleyan University (1920).

HIGHER HIGHER EDUCATION

The Second Great Awakening was qualitatively different from the first theologically. The First was primarily Reformed in the nature of its preaching, teaching, and constituencies. Calvinism was the dominant worldview. In the Second, a major portion of the impact was Wesleyan. The First was focused on justification by grace through faith. In the Second the emphasis was on justification and sanctification, both by grace through faith. The Methodist emphasis on holiness made the character of religious life in the United States different. Initially it would be significant in shaping the nature of Methodist colleges, universities, and seminaries as they were founded.

> As the culture of the nation changed, so did the nature of higher education institutions, including an estrangement of faith and learning, the rift between church and academy, and the separation of personal piety from the quest for academic excellence.

So many founders of Methodist colleges were holiness preachers and teachers. They were spiritually formed in the crucibles of holiness teaching and preaching during the nineteenth century's Second Great Awakening. They included Samuel Logan Brengle, the holiness preacher of the late nineteenth century and early twentieth century Salvation Army, B. T. Roberts, founder of Roberts Wesleyan College, and John Wesley Hughes, the founder of Asbury University, to name a few. While Brengle did not found a college, he can be credited with shaping how the Army's holiness doctrine is taught today in the Army's fifty plus colleges around the world and in its holiness institutes worldwide established in Brengle's name. Likewise, the creation of eleven colleges and universities in the nation by the Nazarene church throughout the twentieth century may be directly attributed to the Wesleyan-Holiness movement that grew out of the great awakening of the twentieth century.

So many Methodist colleges started small and were given initial impetus through the generosity of Methodist businessmen partnering with Methodist bishops, clergy, and lay holiness teachers and preachers. The

A BRIEF HISTORY OF CHRISTIAN HIGHER EDUCATION

holiness movement throughout Methodism fueled and sustained the institutions. In the early years, there was a desire for fidelity to the Wesleyan-Holiness faith commitment to a "full salvation" and a desire to champion the life of the mind through the Christian liberal arts.

As the new nation's colleges and universities grew and matured, many looked to emulate colonial colleges in academic prowess and respectability. It is an old story for both the colonial colleges, now known as Ivy League universities, and the long list of Methodist institutions that today have little or no Christian character. These include universities founded in John Wesley's name: Connecticut Wesleyan, West Virginia Wesleyan, Kentucky Wesleyan, Tennessee Wesleyan, Ohio Wesleyan, Iowa Wesleyan, North Dakota Wesleyan, and so on.

In some cases, formerly Christian institutions maintained a divinity school (Harvard, Yale, Princeton, Vanderbuilt, Duke, Emory, Drew), but the divinity schools were quite separate and isolated from the mainstream academic enterprises of the larger universities. The founding mission, faith commitment, ethos, and worldview of nearly all Methodist colleges and universities, and others of the new nation, can be summed up in two words: dissipation and loss. This is the story of Methodist institutions of higher learning across the nation from Boston University to the University of Southern California.

> As the new nation's colleges and universities grew and matured, many looked to emulate colonial colleges in academic prowess and respectability. It is an old story for both the colonial colleges, now known as Ivy League universities, and the long list of Methodist institutions that today have little or no Christian character.

The eventual dissipation of faith in Christian institutions and their drift away from their Christ-centeredness and missions into secularity is not something that happened with the flip of a switch, nor only to Methodist institutions. It transcended denominational boundaries with a broad impact on colleges of the new nation. It was a gradual process, one president, one board of governors/trustees, one hiring of faculty members at a time. The transition was pushed along by several factors within each institution, but the list of factors is similar to all. It includes a quest for prestige, the necessity of financial stability, and the desire to pursue the new and popular model of German research universities, the absence of needed denominational support financially, and the estrangement of the colleges and universities from their denominations and denominational control.

The greatest factor may have been the reality of denominational church control over the institutions coupled with a kind of denominational abandonment of financial support. Colleges and universities drifted from being Christ-centered in identity, mission, and desired ends not because the leaders of the institutions rejected the Christian faith, but because they found themselves in conflict with their denominational leaders and the control of the church over the affairs, curriculum, and hiring practices of the institutions. The college and university leaders believed that their institutions would prosper better without church control and still manage to remain Christ-centered. Instead, institutions drifted from Christ-centeredness to mission centered, from mission centered to Christian morality and values, then to being church related, church tolerant, eventually non-sectarian, and finally to secular.

Decline and Fall

George Marsden in 1991 spoke about the matter of the mystery of Christianity playing a leading role in Western education until a century or so ago, and now being "absolutely alien to the educational enterprise."

> So the story is not simply that of some bad, or naïve, or foolish people deciding to abandon one of the most valuable aspects of the Protestant heritage. Rather it is more a tale of some people recognizing serious problems in relating their heritage to

the modern world. . . .educational leaders (many of whom were faithful Christians) were responding to some extraordinarily difficult dilemmas, and can not entirely be blamed for some of the unintended results of their choices.[5]

Marsden proposed three major forces impacting leadership of the emerging universities and their constituencies that may account for the transition: (1) demands of a technical society; (2) ideological conflicts; and (3) pluralism and related cultural change. These are factors that are still in play today.

In regard to demands of a technical society, clerically controlled, classicist-oriented higher education collapsed with the advent of the twentieth century because of demand for more scientific subjects in curricula. This was in part driven by the emergence of state schools and their orientation toward agricultural and technical education as practical alternatives to the liberal arts. The old clerical guard undermined itself with its traditional classicism, its high degree of church control and dogmatism, and the low level of denominational financial support for their colleges and universities. Institutions that remained under the control of the church were increasingly relegated to a status of irrelevance and amateurism, leaving little room for scholarly specialization, openness, professional progress, and scientific inquiry.

> Over time the nature of modern American society became increasingly diverse and pluralistic. Liberal Protestantism clashed with Christian conservative exclusivism (sectarianism) and succeeded in establishing it as "out of bounds." Secularism took on a moral legitimacy with its concerns about equity, justice, and pluralism. With time, government funding in support of higher education backed away from religion and from what was viewed as sectarian and exclusive religious teaching.

The second factor had an ideological impact on higher education leadership. The belief emerged that to achieve openness, scientific inquiry, and progress in general it would be essential to suspend religious belief and create a harmonious division of labor between science and religion. To be a scholar was to be a specialist freed from outside religious control. According to Marsden, ideology expressed itself in three broad categories: Traditional Protestantism (conservative), Liberal Protestantism, and Secularism. Eventually, the increasing dominance of Liberal Protestantism allied with ideological Secularism formed a prevailing cultural consensus by the post-World War II era. The Pragmatism of the new ideology sealed the dominance of a secular consensus, sweeping nearly all colleges and universities along and creating a new normal in higher education.

> Given the academy's belief of intellectual mediocrity within the church and in leaders of the church, and the established contempt for faith expressed by the intellectual community and its elites, the Christian college and university today must expect continual distrust from the churches and the academy.

The third and most powerful factor in Marsden's analysis is pluralism. Over time the nature of modern American society became increasingly diverse and pluralistic. Liberal Protestantism clashed with Christian conservative exclusivism (sectarianism) and succeeded in establishing it as "out of bounds." Secularism took on a moral legitimacy with its concerns about equity, justice, and pluralism. With time, government funding in support of higher education backed away from religion and from what was viewed as sectarian and exclusive religious teaching.

For all these reasons, Christian faith and religion moved from the center of higher education to the periphery, from dominance to being incidental. More than that, because of an aggressive secularism, any Christian-informed orientation to higher education today is rejected by many in the academy as out of bounds, irrelevant, not worthy of a hearing in the university context. Methodist institutions certainly did not escape these forces.

A BRIEF HISTORY OF CHRISTIAN HIGHER EDUCATION

Following on the heels of Marsden, in two back-to-back papers, James Tunstead Burtchaell documents a powerful example of "The Decline and Fall of the Christian College." In the first paper he goes into detail with Vanderbuilt University as his centerpiece example.[6] In the second article, he recounts "how the process of estrangement between Vanderbuilt University and the Southern Methodist Church was typical of the alienation of mainstream Protestant colleges and universities from their churches" from 1870 to 1910. He notes that the same process of estrangement took place among American Catholic colleges and universities from 1950 to 1990.[7]

Burchaell leads off his story by citing a litany of quotes that together tell the sad story of the decline:

> Everyone shall consider the main End of his life and studies, to know God and Jesus Christ which is eternal life. John 17:3.
> —*Harvard College, 1646*

> All scholars shall live religious, godly and blameless lives according to the Rules of God's Word, diligently reading the holy Scriptures, the Fountain of Light and Truth; and constantly attend upon all the Duties of Religion both in Publick and Secret.
> —*Yale Laws, 1745*

> A university cannot be built upon a sect.
> —*Charles W. Eliot, Harvard president, 1876.*

> I have watched so many small colleges sucked down the drain by specious appeals to "liberal values" and "top drawer scholarship," as though one cannot find excellent teachers who are also Christians. It is no longer possible to believe that the great central values of Christendom will so commend themselves to

the wise and just as to survive without special and even to some degree coercive nurture.

—*William Muehl, 1975*

Of particular note is Burchaell's observation that the initial leadership of the estranged colleges and universities across the board were devoted Christians in a particular cultural context. It was a context featuring the assumption that the Christian culture would not change and that the institutions would maintain their Christian character while upgrading their academic prowess. Instead, in liberating their institutions from denominational governance and control, the reformers, over time alienated from the churches, occasioned the eventual estrangement from communal "faith seeking understanding." The seeds of a broad dissipation of personal faith and devotion to founding missions were planted and well watered over time.

One of Burchaell's conclusions is that the legacy of estrangement brought with it an antipathy. Given the academy's belief of intellectual mediocrity within the church and in leaders of the church, and the established contempt for faith expressed by the intellectual community and its elites, the Christian college and university today must expect continual distrust from the churches and the academy.

CHAPTER FOUR

NOT ALL CHRISTIANS THINK ALIKE

Adorn the doctrine of God our Savior in all things. Titus 2:10

Methodist denominations, colleges and universities were not alone in the negative change in their characters. The forces and factors that occasioned the shift and drift from foundational moorings impacted Presbyterian, Baptist, Congregational, Anglican, and Catholic institutions alike, with variations in the histories of individual institutions. Nevertheless, out of the broad, sweeping, transformational context of Christian higher education into secularity there arose a fourth wave of Christian colleges and universities.

The Fourth Wave: Christian Colleges and Universities Today
Around the time of and following the American Civil War, a fourth wave of Christian higher education began to emerge. Geneva College was founded

by Presbyterians in 1848. Wheaton College was founded by Methodists in 1860 and soon after became independent and multi-denominational. For the subsequent one hundred and fifty plus years, fourth wave colleges remained faithful to their original character and mission. Their story is the story of several other institutions within and beyond the Wesleyan-Holiness camp.

> The prevailing worldview, theological underpinnings, core curriculum, and orientation toward campus life reflect a diversity of commitments and settled views about what Christian higher education is and what it should achieve.

The third wave of Christian institutions (1790–1900) continued their estrangement from founding denominations and the drift into secularism. A fourth wave, however, began following the American Civil War. Some schools make up a long list of intentionally Christ-centered Christian colleges and universities founded in the later nineteenth and early twentieth centuries by a diversity of denominations including, Church of Christ, Church of God, Church of God (Anderson), Free Methodist, Wesleyan Church, Baptists, Presbyterians, Friends (Quaker), Christian Church, Anabaptists, Pietist, Wesleyans, Nazarenes, and others. They include Milligan College (1866), Calvin College (1976), George Fox (1885), Asbury University (1890), Seattle Pacific University (1891), and Point Loma Nazarene (1902) and a longer list of over one hundred institutions. What they have in common today is that they retain their Christ-centered orientation to higher education. Many institutions began as Bible schools and/or seminaries and transitioned into the Christian liberal arts.

Given the theological diversity of the founding denominations, it is safe to say that not all faculty, leaders, and graduates of fourth-wave institutions think alike. The views of Christian higher education are as varied between institutions as between their founding denominations. The prevailing worldview, theological underpinnings, core curriculum, and orientation toward campus life reflect a diversity of commitments and settled views about what Christian higher education is and what it should achieve. While the second and third waves of higher education marched lockstep into the valley of secularism, the fourth wave appears to have maintained higher ground in keeping fidelity to Christ at the center of the enterprise, but through a diversity of expressions.

Fidelity and Unity in the CCCU

Most of the Christ-centered institutions of the fourth wave share a common ground and unity of convictions through their membership in the Council of Christian Colleges and Universities (CCCU). The CCCU exists to "advance the cause of Christ-centered education and help its institutions transform lives by faithfully relating scholarship and service to biblical truth." It is a broad enough mission statement to be inclusive of a diversity of institutions within the broad tent of evangelical Christianity.

To put this into context, there are over 4,000 higher education institutions granting degrees in the United States. One thousand six hundred (40%) are private, nonprofit institutions of which 900 (10.5%) are self-defined as religiously affiliated. Of those, 120 are intentionally Christ-centered institutions in the U. S. and have qualified for membership according to CCCU requirements. CCCU membership requires certain essentials. An institution must:

> For many, the path to respectability may have been traveled at the cost of losing faith distinctives. In short, they may now be more market driven than mission driven.

- Offer comprehensive undergraduate curricula rooted in the arts and sciences.

- Be located in North America.

- Have non-probationary regional accreditation (U.S. campuses only).

- Have a public, board-approved institutional mission or purpose statement that is Christ-centered and rooted in the historic Christian faith.

- Reflect an integration of scholarship, biblical faith and service in their curricular and extra-curricular programs.

- Hire as full-time faculty members and administrators only persons who profess faith in Jesus Christ.

- Have been, are now, and will continue to be supportive of other Christian colleges.

- Have a commitment to advance the cause of Christian higher education through active participation in the programs of the Council.

- Demonstrate responsible financial operations.

- Have institutional practices which reflect high ethical standards.

- Conduct fundraising activities in a manner consistent with the standards of the Evangelical Council for Financial Accountability.[8]

To carry out its mission and assist its membership, the CCCU provides more than one hundred programs and services. Its work provides a fabric of collegial solidarity and unity among its members. It makes possible a united front in addressing issues of national policy in higher education, the exchange of ideas and resources among members, and social/political/cultural support for a shared mission within the larger context of higher education.

As a reflection of the nature of the fourth wave, the CCCU is a major contributor to the vitality of Christian higher education in the U.S. today and a key factor in the fidelity of its members to their foundational missions. Nevertheless, not all Christians think alike; consequently, not all members of the CCCU offer the same kind of Christian higher education.

> The broadening of mission and vision for many institutions was influenced more by culture than by theologically grounded intention. Along the way for many institutions, there has been a diminishment of commitment to realities of the Christian faith, to higher education as discipleship, and to the development of godly Christian leaders for service and mission.

Not All Christians Think Alike

The Council of Christian Colleges and Universities is a living reminder of Augustine of Hippo's proclamation: "In essentials, unity; in non-essentials, liberty; in all things, charity." The remarkable strength of the CCCU is its unity in the essentials. It requires a foundational commitment to the liberal arts and the basic characteristics of a generic evangelicalism. In a context of collegiality and mutual acceptance and support, theological distinctives are set aside as non-essentials for the sake of unity and the achievement of the common good. But, not all Christians think alike and the member institutions of the CCCU and their respective approaches to higher education reflect that theological diversity.

In *Models for Christian Higher Education: Strategies for Success in the Twenty-first Century,* Richard Hughes and William Adrian highlight the theological diversity of Christian higher education. They present the field in seven camps: Roman Catholic, Lutheran, Mennonite,

Evangelical/Interdenominational, Wesleyan/Holiness, and the Baptist and Restorationist traditions. The theological tradition characteristic of each of these camps shapes the way institutions within think of higher education and pursue it. By way of essays from authors of each of the seven areas, Hughes and Adrian succeed in highlighting how it is possible for a diversity of institutions to develop high quality educational enterprises while nurturing their foundational faith commitments in creative ways.

Nevertheless, there are canaries in the coal mine of Christian higher education and some of those are Wesleyan-Holiness canaries. William Adrian captures a litany of concerns regarding the historical development of Christian institutions of higher learning. The overarching concern is the broadening of their scope and vision both academically and religiously. Specifically:

1. Denominational identities have become less noticeable. Religious activities and observances on campus are increasingly optional.

2. The emphasis on particular religious doctrines are less and less frequently reflected in institutional literature, catalogs, and on web sites.

3. Religious symbols and visual evidence of a Christian presence and spiritual milieu are less apparent.

4. There is a greater emphasis on ecumenism and a diminished emphasis on the institutions' heritages and theological distinctives.

5. There is a general broadening of the curriculum, including professional courses and programs, while there are fewer religion courses and religion faculty. In some cases, religion courses have

been integrated into courses on social issues, ethics, and Western Civilization, peace, justice, and ecology. Faculty positions in religion (biblical and theological studies) are reprogrammed into areas of professional studies to make possible needed budget savings.

6. Many Protestant institutions founded on a particular faith tradition with specific theological distinctives have broadened their approach to the market and their vision of the future by embracing an evangelical identity.

7. The trend in the CCCU orbit of Christian higher education has been expansion of members' academic programs into full-blown universities offering undergraduate and graduate degrees. They have pursued the establishment of professional schools of business, nursing, law, psychology, kinesiology, and others. Much of the broadening of scope and vision, programs and degree offerings, reflect quality institutions of higher learning that have passed the phase of survival to become regionally and nationally recognized and respected. For many, the path to respectability may have been traveled at the cost of losing faith distinctives. In short, Adrian suggests that they may now be more market driven than mission driven.

It is understandable that Christian higher education is being in part or in whole driven by the market for several reasons:

1. For a long time, these institutions operated in the survival mode, totally dependent on student tuition. The new normal emerged so that financial resources became the highest priority and theological distinctives were sacrificed and downplayed.

2. As denominational support diminished in the way of funding and the supply of students, schools expanded their market by appealing to a broader constituency. The same was true for recruiting faculty.

3. As academic credentials required doctorates and publications, in part for achieving regional accreditation of institutions, and as institutions grew in their programs and degree offerings, it became more difficult to secure faculty. A broadening of the faculty influenced a broadening of what was taught and the perspectives that carried the curriculum. Both students and faculty came from an increasingly diverse theological landscape.

4. The broadening of mission and vision for many institutions was influenced more by culture than by theologically grounded intention. Along the way for many institutions, there has been a diminishment of commitment to realities of the Christian faith, to higher education as discipleship, and to the development of godly Christian leaders for service and mission.

In a subsequent work, Richard T. Hughes gives the reader his reflections on faith and scholarship in *How Christian Faith Can Sustain the Life of the Mind*.

In particular, Hughes counters the widespread misperception of Christian dogmatism and narrowness. He makes the case that, when faith is pursued, it can nourish openness and curiosity. Hughes gives a strong, robust assessment of how Christian faith can strengthen scholarship and teaching by sustaining the life of the mind. He does this by considering four different Christian traditions—Catholic, Reformed, Anabaptist, and Lutheran and the different ways they contribute to the life of the mind. Unfortunately, he does not engage the Wesleyan-Holiness tradition, leaving the task to another. Many Wesleyan-Holiness denominations remain financially challenged and incapable of significant financial support of their colleges and universities. Consequently, most Wesleyan-Holiness heritage institutions operate on a very thin financial margin while striving to provide a high quality academic experience.

CHAPTER FIVE

THE REMNANT IN THE WESLEYAN-HOLINESS CONTEXT

Let us keep our eyes fixed on Jesus, on whom our faith depends from beginning to end.

Hebrews 12:2

The history of the rise and fall of Christian higher education in America through the nineteenth and first half of the twentieth centuries has its exceptions. Following the American Civil War, within the Wesleyan-Holiness tradition there arose colleges and universities with a sustained fidelity to their denominations and holiness-tethered missions. They are a remnant of early American Methodism with roots back to John Wesley and the Methodist movement to "spread scriptural holiness throughout the land." This remnant is largely outside of mainstream Methodism represented today by the United Methodist Church whose colleges and universities went down the path of denominational estrangement, faith dissipation, and secularism.

For many years, the remnant colleges within Wesleyan-Holiness constituencies maintained their connectivity to their founding denominations, many of which were reform movements within American Methodism. These denominations include the Free Methodist Church, Wesleyan Church, Church of God (Anderson), Brethren in Christ, Christian Missionary Alliance, Church of the Nazarene, The Salvation Army, the Shield of Faith, and several others which today are active in the Wesleyan-Holiness Consortium.

> Like their colleague institutions in the CCCU, colleges and universities of Wesleyan-Holiness heritage are broadening in scope, downplaying distinctive theological doctrines, and hiring more and more widely from outside their traditions. They increasingly recruit students and faculty from other evangelical constituencies and enroll students from the general public who are seeking a high-quality education in a "safe" setting.

The colleges and universities that these denominations founded worked at staying close to their denominational moorings. Today they represent varying degrees of fidelity to a Wesleyan-Holiness commitment, and yet they represent a drift in the direction of generic evangelicalism and secularism. Like their colleague institutions in the CCCU, colleges and universities of Wesleyan-Holiness heritage are broadening in scope, downplaying distinctive theological doctrines, and hiring more and more widely from outside their traditions. They increasingly recruit students and faculty from other evangelical constituencies and enroll students from the general public who are seeking a high-quality education in a "safe" setting.

Boards of Trustees and Governors understandably continue to look to senior leadership in presidents with business experience and credentials and fundraising strength. Increasingly, presidents have little orientation to

THE REMNANT IN THE WESLEYAN-HOLINESS CONTEXT

or appreciation for the Wesleyan theological distinctives of the institution. In some cases, they are hired from outside the primary denominational constituencies of Wesleyan-Holiness.

The Past as Prologue to the Future

Colleges and universities with Wesleyan-Holiness heritage find themselves in the same place that Christian higher education has faced for the past four hundred years. The obvious question begs an answer. Is the past inevitably prologue to the future? Is the future inevitably a slow slide from Christ-centerdness, from Holy Spirit empowered and guided fidelity to a predestined secularism?

Not long ago I found myself at the helm of an outstanding Christian university. Its remarkable faculty, academic programs, and first-rate student life programing became well integrated. Their forte' was promoting not merely a quality academic experience for students, but a trajectory of educational vitality that included a remarkable degree of spiritual maturity of the students upon graduation. In my forty years in higher education, twenty-four in Christian higher education, I've not seen a more splendid capacity for student transformation. Nevertheless, two realities continue to present the potential for either the eventual drift into secularism or ascendency to a higher level of transformation and impact. Wesleyan-Holiness heritage institutions are vulnerable to the former and well positioned for the latter.

In the first reality, the potential for an eventual drift into secularism, it became clear that within the university not everyone was on the same page regarding the university's identity, mission, and ultimate *raison d'etre*. When I began my work there, I assumed everyone thought like I did. I assumed that the whole university existed for the whole person, starting with its Christ-centeredness. In the heart of a Christ-centered college or university, the essence of the institution is Christ. His Spirit, the Holy Spirit, resident in every faculty and staff member, is to be a palpable reality. By His Spirit and their consecration, the Word becomes flesh in all those who sign on to the mission of the university. Christ is present in the life of the university community and is at the center of all that takes place. The Spirit of Christ in us, the Holy Spirit, is the essence of the university. Christ is the permeating nature and presence, Emmanuel, God with us.

In my naiveté I was quite surprised to discover that some faculty and staff were not there. Instead of being Christo-centric, they were mission centric. That's great, but it's not the same. Well-articulated missions can inspire and rally people to achieve great things. But mission statements are words. Christ at the center is the incarnational life of the enterprise. Others were very Christian worldview centric, especially in the humanities. This is powerful in its impact within a core curriculum in the liberal arts. But, a Christian worldview must be centered in Christ as distinctive from all other perspectives. Still others, especially in the professional schools, were centered in Christian values. "Values at work" became a pragmatic and dominant viewpoint. Still others were very denominationally centered with concerns that the university have strong representation of their particular church constituencies in the student enrollment, faculty hiring, university leadership, and membership on the Board of Governors.

The Drift Off-Center

While president, I believed and preached that a Christian university must be and remain Christo-centric, centered in Christ. As the motto of Wheaton College proclaims, its commitment must be "Christ Pre-eminent." In this particular case, this wonderful university was already slipping. The point of its compass in key places was drifting from the still-point of Jesus, who is to be the essence of the university, its nature and being. In some quarters it had slipped to the mission, shifting from who the university is in Christ to what it does. In some quarters, a perspective was the priority, the Christian

THE REMNANT IN THE WESLEYAN-HOLINESS CONTEXT

worldview. It was presented as an attractive alternative to the worldviews of other religions and secularity. It was a step to acknowledging the relativity of the Christian perspective among others.

Christian values at the center of the enterprise moves the point of the compass even further from Christ as the center. Christian values are articulated in words and viewed as similar to other philosophies and religions. They articulate principles very similar to non-Christian values. Finally, church affiliation and representation is just one step from secularism. Most secular institutions today, which arose from the Wesleyan-Holiness heritage, still have ties to Methodism through endowments, token board representation, and most importantly on-campus ministries from formerly constituent churches. Nevertheless, they are secular and far from their roots and original convictions.

If a college or university is off-centered and does not remain Christ-centered, it will eventually dissipate in its commitments and distinctives. It will drift into an eventual secularism. However, if it remains Christ-centered, it can provide the world with a vibrant mission, a powerful Christian worldview through the eyes of Christ, robust Christian values to live by, and exemplary and supportive relations with the primary denominational constituencies. It can do all those things. It need not dissipate in faith or drift into a predetermined secularism.

For the Wesleyan-Holiness heritage institutions today, the drift off-center is underway. The forces pulling the CCCU institutions away from their historic moorings are powerful. Members of the Wesleyan-Holiness heritage are no exception. The mutually supportive fabric of the CCCU members serves to buffer the forces of secularization, but the pull is still there, strong and persistent. At the same time, the theological distinctives of CCCU schools are subtly drifting into a generic evangelicalism.

The signs and indicators of off-centered drift toward secularism, dissipation of faith, and loss of theological distinctives are there. The abiding questions include, "What are we to do?" "How did we get here?" "How do we affirm our holiness heritage and at the same time strengthen the institution?" Again, two realities present the potential for either the eventual drift into secularism or ascendency to a higher level of transformation and impact. To embrace an ascendency will mean an honest critique of our history of the American holiness movement and the impact from Wesleyan churches and colleges initially.

The way Wesleyan-Holiness experience is conceived today was framed long ago in the roots of the holiness movement. Is it too bold to say that the history of the holiness movement promoted a flawed, distorted, and incomplete idea of the holiness experience? If so, then the prevailing idea of holiness makes it difficult for colleges and universities to promote an educational experience of consecration and sanctification. When our historical way of thinking about our holiness heritage is corrected, is it possible to return to our original theological roots and find there a way forward to embrace holiness as the ultimate student outcome? In this way, can we raise the bar of excellence in higher education to a pinnacle not seen before? How might the priorities in our approach to holiness in higher education provide a way forward? The renewal of our Wesleyan-Holiness thinking and priorities, and the way forward, is the focus of this book's Part Two.

PART TWO

CHAPTER SIX

A HERITAGE OF HOLINESS

God has not called us to uncleanness, but to holiness.
1 Thessalonians 4:7

The remnant of Wesleyan-Holiness heritage colleges and universities shares common ground. John Wesley is their father. On the one hand, the heritage they share is a marvelously balanced, integrated understanding of scriptural holiness. On the other hand, they also share an historical tragedy occasioned by the crisis-oriented paradigm of American revivalism.

John Wesley's Theology of Holiness

John Wesley's mission was to spread holiness throughout the land. For him, holiness was key to understanding both justification and sanctification. He understood salvation to be possible through the gracious prevenient work of God's grace bringing people to faith, first in justification and then sanctification. Wesley's message was one of holiness of heart and life. He taught and preached that we can be saved from our sins (justification), and saved to Christ's likeness and therefore purity of heart (sanctification).

For Wesley this was a full salvation by the grace of God from sin to the restoration of the image of God in us. He was an optimist. He understood that God's grace makes possible a pragmatic optimism. No matter how sinful and far from God someone may be, salvation from the penalty and guilt of sin is possible. Even more, salvation in the form of restoration to the likeness of Christ and sanctification is also possible. This two-fold salvation from sin and to holiness, from the guilt and penalty of sin to power over sin, makes possible a purity of the heart that benefits the whole individual and the world overall.

> Christian higher education ideally produces well-educated disciples who reproduce disciples and impact the world for Christ. Overwhelmingly, the potential of Wesleyan-Holiness higher education to multiply and spread scriptural holiness across the land did not happen. Instead, holiness teaching transitioned into dogmatic and legalistic doctrine. It lost its appeal, especially in the context of colleges and universities devoted to the liberal arts.

The theology of Wesley was balanced and integrated. It was conjunctive, both/and. It proclaimed both justification and sanctification, both from sin and to restoration, both rescue from perishing and transformation into holiness and purity of heart. He presented an optimistic theology of progression, a *via salutis*. That is to say, Wesley promoted a way of salvation out of the darkness of sin and separation from God and into the light of a glorious intimacy with God. Wesley's theological framework assumed a synergism between God and humankind. He understood God's grace to be lavishly poured out to us, a grace that calls for a response.

Wesley's is a theology of dynamic, interactive relationship of God and humankind. Sin separates us from God. The sacrifice of Christ on the cross and his victory over death made it possible for us to be reconciled with God. Reconciliation positions us to have a growing, increasingly intimate relationship with God contingent on our continuing obedient response to God's continuing grace.

In Wesley's treatise *A Plain Account of Christian Perfection*[9] he presents his views at length. After conversion, God continues his work of grace. Through the growing, interactive relationship, God calls us to live a Christlike life of holiness with him. Where there is a response to God's grace of total consecration on our part, God responds with more grace through the Holy Spirit to sanctify us, purifying us and perfecting our intention and capacity to love God and others. Such sanctification Wesley described as Christian perfection. The way of salvation for Wesley is the journey of being perfected. It is the ongoing walk with God in which exposures to the varied forms of divine grace grows our hearts in capacity to be "filled to the measure of the fullness of God" (Eph. 3:19).

Another way to say this is that in the Christian journey there are exposures to the varied means by which God pours grace into our lives. Those exposures include time spent in reading and meditating on God's Word, time in prayer both personal and corporate, absorbing Christian literature that aids reflection on scripture and others' Christian experience, the testimony of others, and Christian fellowship—to mention just a few. Wesley taught the importance of the means of grace in the Christian life.

In his book *The Presence of God in the Christian Life: John Wesley and the Means of Grace*,[10] Henry Knight suggests that the means of grace do two things key in the process of forming and deepening of our relationship with God. They help us experience God's presence and clarify God's identity. In this way they promote the social (dynamic, interactive, synergistic) nature of our relationship with God. Wesley's theology is highly relational. At its heart is the idea of obedience to the Great Commandment to love God and neighbor. It implies that the process of a growing relationship with God is possible, even an intimate one.

HIGHER HIGHER EDUCATION

Implicit in a Wesleyan theology of holiness is a journey with God characterized by a process of increasing intimacy through exposures to God's means of grace. Through God's means we experience his presence and see ever more clearly who God is. God is self-revealing. In the process of a growing faith where there are exposures to God's grace there will be encounters with God. These encounters are crises of illumination, compassion, and cleansing. They occasion moments of sanctification. Wesley's theology is both process and crisis, exposures and encounters. It is not either/or, but rather both/and.

> American revivalism occasioned a serious weakening of the ability of Wesleyan-Holiness institutions to promote an understanding and embrace of full salvation in ways that permeated the curriculum and impacted student outcomes, faculty scholarship, and institutional fidelity to its theological underpinnings.

Wesley's theology, then, is a lively, healthy, and comprehensive vision of the Christian life. Historically, it fit the upbeat, optimistic energy of the new nineteenth-century American nation. As the nation grew and moved westward, Methodism grew. It expanded into every nook and cranny of the emerging nation. I am told that today there is an expression of Methodism in every county of the United States and that at one time where one would find a post office one would also find a Methodist church. With the advance of Methodism came the preaching and teaching of Wesley's emphasis on a full salvation, the idea of growth in grace, and spiritual progress and formation in holiness.

Initially, the Methodist pastors and lay preachers carried the message of a full salvation. With the founding of colleges, universities and seminaries, the Wesleyan-Holiness teaching of both process and crisis had the potential to be taken to another level. Higher education is an act of multiplication. It produces graduates of competence who impact society. Christian higher education ideally produces well-educated disciples who reproduce disciples and impact the world for Christ. Overwhelmingly, the potential of Wesleyan-Holiness higher education to multiply and spread scriptural holiness across the land did not happen. Instead, holiness teaching transitioned into dogmatic and legalistic doctrine. It lost its appeal, especially in the context of colleges and universities devoted to the liberal arts.

In time, the teaching and preaching of a theology of holiness became increasingly varied. Interpretations, emphases, and nuances occasioned or followed various denominational splits in Methodism. Lines were drawn. Boundaries worked against unity and promoted exclusion. Ironically, a theology one might expect to bring unity instead promoted diversity with departures from the theology first espoused by John Wesley.

The Crisis Orientation of American Revivalism

American revivalism knocked Wesleyan-Holiness off balance. No more serious a departure took place than that unintentionally promoted by the nature of American revivalism of the nineteenth and early twentieth centuries. The nature of higher education in Wesleyan-Holiness colleges and institutions was directly impacted by this departure.

In some ways it was a false start. As a result, a theology of holiness was never successfully integrated into the mission, goals, and vision of the respective Wesleyan-Holiness institutions of higher learning. Holiness became an add-on, a fringe benefit, but not central to the educational outcomes to which institutions were devoted. American revivalism occasioned a serious weakening of the ability of Wesleyan-Holiness institutions to promote an understanding and embrace of full salvation in ways that permeated the curriculum and impacted student outcomes, faculty scholarship, and institutional fidelity to its theological underpinnings.

The genius of John Wesley was his ability to integrate aspects of Christianity and theology that were historically disjointed. He was gifted at holding things in creative tension. This included "knowledge and vital piety," piety and social concerns, justification and sanctification, faith and works, small accountability groups and the institutional church, spiritual formation and evangelism, crisis and process. His theology of holiness rested squarely on the careful balance of process and crisis, growth through exposures to grace and direct encounters with a holy God. American revivalism upset the balance of process and crisis by its strong, evangelical emphasis on a crisis experience, not only in justification (initial salvation) but also in subsequent entire sanctification.

In Wesley's ministry the success of the small group class meetings resulted in weekly exposures to the means of prevenient grace. The composition of the small groups included converted and unconverted members. In the process of exposures to scripture, prayer, testimony, loving kindness and support, and other means of grace, hundreds of thousands of persons came to faith and grew in faith through continued exposures (process). Moments of crisis in repentance and redemption were preceded by the preparation of the soil into which the seed of the gospel could take root. In American revivalism, the whole process was increased in its temporal dimension. The frontier revivals and revival camp meetings condensed the whole experience into one revival meeting or into a short series of meetings. It was salvation on the fast track, with the goal of getting as many people "saved" and "sanctified" as quickly as possible.

> The tragedy in the history of Christian higher education, and especially for Wesleyan-Holiness institutions, is the loss of opportunity for the university or college to facilitate for its students the highest spiritual end. The bias of holiness as a crisis experience has blocked Christian higher education from seeking holiness through the balance of process and crisis experiences designed to lead toward desired student outcomes.

The crisis-oriented revival meeting became the dominant paradigm. It even impacted how faith communities came together for regular worship. Many Wesleyan-Holiness denominations gathered for worship on Sunday mornings with holiness as the focus and on Sunday evenings with evangelistic outreach as the focus. In both cases, the altar call for sanctification and salvation from sin was fashioned after the likeness of revival meetings. Everything in the worship service led up to the altar call where there could be a crisis experience of justification or sanctification. This is not to say that there was something wrong with altar calls or staging opportunities for God to speak in a special way at a special time in a call to salvation or holiness. It is to say that there is something missing when the process is not one of continuing growth. Instead, one is left to the pressure cooker of revivals and Sunday meetings.

American evangelicalism promoted the same crisis experience for holiness as for evangelism. The balance of holiness as both process and crisis was lost to holiness as only a crisis experience. It was promoted in a form of quick and pressured commitment at the altar in the context of a meeting designed to bring about that particular crisis experience. Over the years, great good has been done in bringing people to the point of decision and faith, and also to commitments to a deeper relationship with God in holiness. But this good came with considerable loss. The paradigm of pressure-cooker evangelism has all but disappeared in the present day. It still exists in many Wesleyan-Holiness churches in the form of the annual revival meeting which lasts a week.

In short, the balance that John Wesley brought to a full salvation as both process and crisis was upset. The steady impact of patient processes, of daily exposures and reflection, leading to insight and commitment was largely lost. The prevenient grace preparing the soil for the full gospel of salvation and sanctification was no longer supplied as an intentional strategy. It is interesting to note that many Wesleyan-Holiness colleges and institutions originally incorporated Wesley's small class meetings into the student experience, but by the 1950s that practice died out. It is no wonder that Christian higher education adopted the American revivalism/crisis paradigm for holiness.

The second tragedy of American revivalism, then, is that it framed holiness contrary to the nature of higher education. As a crisis paradigm, it failed to take root. It was antithetical to the process-oriented nature of higher education. Education does not occur as episodic crises. Education is a process. It entails a sustained series of exposures, the emergence of insights, and the internalization of knowledge. It doesn't happen in a pressure cooker of crises.

Nevertheless, Christian colleges and universities, including those of the Wesleyan-Holiness heritage, were stuck with the evangelism paradigm of faith experience being fostered in crisis-oriented altar calls. What could they do with that educationally? It doesn't lend itself to inclusion in the curriculum. Instead it lends itself to inclusion in the college calendar as the college's annual revival. You won't find it in the classroom. You may find it in the college chapel. Crisis management of faith became a programmed, add-on activity, an extra-curricular reality not central to the mission of the college or university. Today it remains an optional extra, but not an essential.

The tragedy in the history of Christian higher education, and especially for Wesleyan-Holiness institutions, is the loss of opportunity for the university or college to facilitate for its students the highest spiritual end. If Wesley's balance were to be maintained, the potential for the presence of God in the student's life and in the lives of all faculty and staff would be unimaginable. Higher education is all about process leading to outcomes. Wesley's theology of holiness is all about a process that leads to outcomes. Higher education provides an intentional program of exposures with the goal of the transformation of the student. Wesleyan-Holiness does the same. Higher education promotes the integration of learning across subject areas and domains of inquiry. Wesleyan-Holiness promotes faith and learning toward growth and spiritual maturity.

Higher education seeks knowledge that is internalized and produces wisdom. Holiness does the same, producing the wisdom of a pure heart.

A HERITAGE OF HOLINESS

The tragedy is that until now the processes leading to deeper spirituality and holiness have not been optimally integrated into the curricula of Wesleyan-Holiness colleges and universities. The bias of holiness as a crisis experience has blocked Christian higher education from seeking holiness through the balance of process and crisis experiences designed to lead toward desired student outcomes. This now frames the challenge of our finding a way to go forward from where we are now.

The third tragedy of American revivalism is its exclusive emphasis on crises of the heart. The unfortunate impact in Wesleyan higher education is that an emphasis on a crisis of the heart without the process of developing head and heart together runs contrary to a concern for whole person development. It sets the stage for a fragmentation of head, heart, and life. A crisis approach to holiness is understood as a matter of the heart and with a changed heart a changed life. Christian higher education, with its emphasis on educational process, customarily left crises of the heart to the extra-curricular activities of annual college revivals and chapels. In doing this it also made the pursuit of holiness not a shared priority of the whole university community, but rather an episodic event scheduled by campus ministry. Herein, holiness is undervalued and disengaged as a social/relational undertaking of the campus community. The extra-curricular orientation of a crisis approach isolates and fragments holiness from the overarching mission of the institution.

> Colleges and universities in the Wesleyan tradition are well placed to bring head, heart, and life together within a heightened appreciation of its heritage as initially conceived by John Wesley.

To this day, higher education is normatively understood as a cognitive exercise only. As one president of a large, public university said, "The purpose of a university is the acquisition and dissemination of knowledge," nothing more.[11] Christian higher education institutions have bought into this grossly limited idea of higher education. The prevailing secular thought is that higher education has a social reality. Societies create and support colleges and universities for social, civil, and economic reasons, anticipating positive impacts on the lives of others. There is a practical concern with ethics and with what is right for others. This secular perspective misses the fact that higher education is also a matter of the heart and life.

For Wesleyan-Holiness colleges and universities, higher education can be even higher when the educational exposures over time help students integrate matters of the head, heart, and life. An education is more than head knowledge. The Apostle Paul makes this clear when he prays that the Ephesians will be so rooted and established in love that they may know Christ's love "that surpasses knowledge" (Eph. 3:19a). Paul is saying that there is a knowledge that integrates the head and the heart, and such knowledge can bring us to a crisis experience of being "filled to the measure of the fullness of God," holiness (Eph. 3:19b).

Wesley was fond of saying that there is no holiness outside of social holiness. This rings true in how holiness unfolds and in how it is lived out in daily life in its relational impact on others. Christian universities and colleges are powerful social, relational contexts, or social/spiritual ecologies if you will, filled with the potential of exposures that integrate head, heart, and life.

In conventional higher education, there is little room for the education of the heart. Colleges and universities in the Wesleyan tradition are well placed to bring head, heart, and life together within a heightened appreciation of its heritage as initially conceived by John Wesley. This means a balanced approach to the curriculum by the integration of the means of grace into the student experience. It means not leaving it to chapel, Bible studies in the residence halls, or to the expensive, occasional missions tourism to exotic places.

A curriculum is possible that intentionally produces godly graduates who walk in holiness, whose daily walk brings them into closer and closer intimacy with God, and who are filled to the measure of the fullness of

God. It is not surprising that the Apostle Paul moves from Ephesians 3:19 and the fullness of God to 3:20 and God's ability to "do immeasurably more than we ask or imagine." The "immeasurably more" is in the context of and contingent on the "fullness of God" in the Christian's life.

The ultimate proclamation of this book is that it is possible to rethink Christian higher education in ways that balance head, heart, and life. It is possible to offer a higher form of higher education that balances process and crisis in spiritual maturity and purity of heart. In so doing, it is possible for colleges and universities in the Wesleyan-Holiness tradition to reclaim their full heritage in ways that transform *higher* education into *highest* education. It doesn't mean that all the forces and challenges won't still be pressing on the institution: finances, enrollment, student recruitment, government regulations and relations, preventive maintenance needs, faculty recruitment and development, etc. The list will always be there.

What then does it mean? It does mean getting more bang for the dollars invested by multiplication. Higher education relies on the multiplier effect. The degree of impact on graduates will result in their impact on others who then impact others. Reclaiming a balanced Wesleyan heritage can take the institution to unprecedented levels of mission achievement and to a new pinnacle of *higher* higher education.

CHAPTER SEVEN

RECLAIMING THE HERITAGE

The splendor of holiness.

Psalm 29:2

Today a mighty river of the Spirit is bursting forth from the hearts of women and men, boys and girls. It is a deep river of divine intimacy, a powerful river of holy living, a dancing river of jubilation in the Spirit, and a broad river of unconditional love for all peoples.

—Richard Foster in ***Streams of Living Waters***

Like the Jordan River south of the Sea of Galilee, one may wonder if the mighty river of the Spirit had dried up in places. If so, what could be done about it? The twenty-first century began with an initiative to revisit and reclaim John Wesley's great passion to "spread scriptural holiness throughout the land." The Wesleyan-Holiness movement cooled and in some respects was dormant. The river ran dry. The truism expressed by Salvation Army founder, William Booth became a reality in Wesleyan quarters. Booth said, "The tendency of fire is to go out." If the fire of holiness teaching, preaching, and living has not gone out, but merely diminished in the Wesleyan-Holiness movement, it seems to be only a flicker and a few embers in the churches and in the colleges and universities of Wesleyan-Holiness heritage. It needs attention. It requires oxygen and fuel if it is to become once again a blazing fire.

An overarching assumption of this writing is that the Wesleyan-Holiness movement, as embraced by its colleges and universities, is more than waning under the sole paradigm of American revivalism and crisis. It will only be rediscovered and revived when institutions reclaim their heritage and commit to a return to Wesley's balance of process *and* crisis. This means pursuing higher education of the whole person by the whole university embracing holiness in student outcomes of the highest spiritual ends, spiritual maturity and purity of heart.

The Wesleyan-Holiness Study Group

Given the present state of affairs within many Wesleyan institutions, scholars from eight historically Wesleyan-Holiness denominations were called together over a period of three years to discuss the idea of holiness.[12] At the end of three years, selected papers from the discussions were shaped into a book.[13] This collection of writings covered topics of holiness in scripture, historical and theological perspectives on holiness, and holiness in ministry. In the appendices of the book, one may find several descriptions of holiness by some of those gathered:

RECLAIMING THE HERITAGE

Roger Green: "I continue to find strength in a definition of holiness as a life of obedience, rooted in love, to the Great Commandment of our Lord—to love God and love our neighbor supremely. Samuel Logan Brengle in his work entitled *The Way of Holiness* wrote that 'Sanctification is to have our sinful tempers cleansed, and the heart filled with love to God and man.' Obedience is the natural outcome of that love for God, and so we are compelled to love our neighbor also. Because holiness is corporate as well as personal, such obedience is to be manifested by the church as well as by individual believers."

Lisa Dorsey: "...there are two natures of holiness, divine and human. Both are essential to the holiness journey ... (which articulates) the progressive nature of holiness . . . the process of this continuing perfection ignited by one's love for Christ.... Hence, holiness is an outward manifestation of the inward work of Christ in the believer for his sovereign purposes."

Craig Keen: "Holiness means, in the first place, what is peculiar to God. It is God's separateness, difference from the world."

Thomas Nobel: "In the Father's heart, then, revealed in Jesus, we see that the eternal holiness of God is not just to be seen negatively as 'separation,' but positively as love, . . . Holiness is pure and perfect love."

Lynn Thrush: ". . . holiness is the good character of God unmixed by any shadow of darkness . . . relational . . . (a call to) all persons to a transformation of life and fullness of God, holiness working in the disciple's life as an ongoing journey of yielding to God and growing in grace."

Throughout the *Holiness Manifesto*, authors of various chapters offer definitions and clarifications of the essence of holiness. Barry Callen wrote, "Holiness is about life being transformed by and in God's Spirit. It is about serious believers in Jesus Christ, who they are, who they are intended to be, who they have actually become, and who they might yet be by the grace of God. It is about forming communities of faith that reflect the Spirit of Christ and are actively about Christ's agenda in the world . . . in short, who will be *like* God as God works redemptively in this world.

Howard Snyder wrote that the call to holiness is a call to Trinitarian love, "the amazing, gracious invitation to 'participate in the divine nature (2 Peter 1:4, NIV)' . . . holiness means sharing the very character of God . . . to pursue what Wesley called 'all inward and outward holiness.'

Two things strike me as I've shared the above regarding the gathering for three years of professors of Christian colleges, universities, and seminaries to discuss holiness. On the one hand, they were not exactly all on the same page nor singing from the same hymnal. It reminds me of the old joke that where you have two faculty you have three opinions. On the other hand, they are all expressing an orientation to holiness within the historical Wesleyan tradition. What is not as well captured in the writings, but was palpable in the discussions of which I took part, was the passion and conviction of the gathered academics regarding the importance of holiness in the Christian life.

> An overarching assumption of this writing is that the Wesleyan-Holiness movement, as embraced by its colleges and universities, is more than waning under the sole paradigm of American revivalism and crisis. It will only be rediscovered and revived when institutions reclaim their heritage and commit to a return to Wesley's balance of process *and* crisis. This means pursuing higher education of the whole person by the whole university embracing holiness in student outcomes of the highest spiritual ends, spiritual maturity and purity of heart.

Even the language used by the gathered academics differed reflecting the preferences of their denominations and their own understanding of the Wesleyan doctrine of holiness. The classical terms for holiness include entire sanctification, Christian perfection, the second blessing, baptism of the Holy Spirit, and the fullness of God. Most of these expressions no longer suffice in capturing the imagination of a new generation other than the practical portrayal of holiness as Christ-likeness. The misunderstood idea of holiness for many persons is aversive because of the immediate assumption of legalism, elitism, and sinless perfection. Holiness is misunderstood as a straightjacket of do's and don'ts, or only for a few who are super Christians. It is viewed as sinless perfection and unachievable no matter how hard one tries.

Clearly, holiness is not well taught or preached. If taught well, people would see the conjunctive nature of God's grace in holiness being on the one hand a work of God alone, and on the other hand a synergistic partnership with God, God's favor and at the same time his empowerment. It is God's gift of grace and a response to the giver, an instantaneous crisis moment and yet an ongoing process. It is personal yet social.[14] It is personal development and dynamic social-spiritual interactionism. Conjunctively, it is the acquaintance process for the individual to know God and the consequential, emergent intimacy with God.

The Wesleyan-Holiness Consortium

The discussions and papers of the Wesleyan-Holiness Study Project laid the foundation for a more visionary, expansive step to reclaim a heritage of holiness for both Wesleyan-Holiness churches and the colleges and universities they founded. Over a period of several years, since its inception in 2002, the Wesleyan-Holiness Consortium has evolved, not as an organization, but as a network of participating churches, denominations, universities, colleges, and other affiliation groups.[15]

While the Wesleyan-Holiness Consortium quickly achieved a measure of sophistication as reflected in the figure below, it remains a humble enterprise guided by the Holy Spirit. The hopes of the collaborative participants are that the WHC will be a means of grace in reclaiming a heritage of holiness within Wesleyan heritage churches, colleges and universities, and others.

The Wesleyan-Holiness Consortium is a result of a sustained vision for renewal of scriptural holiness throughout the land. Several realities come into focus when looking back over the past several years.

1. God is at work renewing his church. *"Behold; I will do a new thing"* (Isaiah 43:19). Where in the church there is atrophy, unraveling, decline, lost ground, diminishment or neglect, God is known to raise up a new, fresh means of grace, a renewed way forward, a reviving of human agency for Kingdom ends.

2. A collective resolve to embrace a vision, take initiative, and provide support was embraced by national, denominational leaders brought together in Dallas, Texas in September 2006 to consider the emergent outcomes of the Wesleyan-Holiness Study Group and to form the Wesleyan-Holiness Consortium. This leadership group agreed to continue the spread of "Scriptural Holiness Across the Land". They did this (1) by facilitating the ongoing theological dialogue among groups with common heritage and a common message; (2) by supporting events that would gather young leaders and others around the idea of holiness; and (3) by encouraging and supporting the multiplication of regional networks, pastor's days, and local summits centering on holiness. They agreed to give themselves to unity within and among participating churches, to lift up a holiness voice to the broader church, and to promote the centrality and missional importance of holiness to the future of the church.

3. There is no master plan. There has been no grand strategy. There is only the ongoing, dynamic of the Holy Spirit's guidance and direction. In that dynamic there is the calling of a growing number of persons to obedience, consecration and fidelity of response to the leading of the Holy Spirit and a reawakening to the rich Wesleyan-Holiness tradition which in both orthodoxy (correct believing), orthopraxy (proper living), and orthopathy (transformed hearts) for the 21st century.

The Wesleyan-Holiness Consortium and Higher Education

In regard to holiness and higher education, it is important to visit two aspects of the WHC. The evolution of the networking movement of the WHC occasioned two innovations for the promotion of Wesleyan-Holiness: The President's Affinity Group and the Aldersgate Press.

The President's Affinity Group. Many of the Wesleyan heritage denominations participating in the regional networks and gatherings of pastors still maintained positive relationships with the colleges and universities they founded. Yet many of these institutions still experience some measure of drift from or partial amnesia regarding their theological heritage. While some remain robust in their Wesleyan theological groundedness, others do not see it as a priority. The vision emerged from the WHC to build on its success with the initial study group and strengthen its ties with its constituent colleges and universities beginning with presidents.

> The classical terms for holiness include entire sanctification, Christian perfection, the second blessing, baptism of the Holy Spirit, and the fullness of God. Most of these expressions no longer suffice in capturing the imagination of a new generation other than the practical portrayal of holiness as Christ-likeness. The misunderstood idea of holiness for many persons is aversive because of the immediate assumption of legalism, elitism, and sinless perfection.

The first WHC meeting of Wesleyan-Holiness college and university presidents took place in January of 2009 in conjunction with the Council of Christian Colleges and Universities meeting in Washington D.C. Sixteen presidents attended. Every year since, the presidents have gathered together prior to the annual presidents' meeting of the CCCU to discuss issues of common interest in reclaiming scriptural holiness in the life of their institutions. The number of institutions on the WHC invitation list for this annual gathering has grown to sixty-three and includes three Canadian and two Latin American institutions. A few chief academic officers were present for the gathering of presidents.

A major theme of the WHC and its meeting of the presidents' affinity group is unity. There is a collegial acknowledgement of the carefully nuanced differences in how institutions and their founding denominations think of holiness and how they interpret John Wesley. Some institutions have a history of rigorous scholarship regarding Wesleyan studies, theology, and its implications for higher education. The Nazarene church affiliated institutions come to mind as an example. Over the years they have invested in maintaining and deepening their roots in the soil of Wesleyan theology with its implications for spiritual formation and the enterprise of higher education. Others have established lecture series and special occasions to celebrate their holiness heritage. Several remain relatively disengaged from their heritage and roots. All presidents come to the table with an interest in hearing and seeing what other institutions are doing. It is a slow process but an important one, given the remarkable potential in the aggregation of these institutions to contribute to Wesley's vision regarding the spread of scriptural holiness in the future and the potential for many to reclaim a partially lost heritage.

A newer development with exciting potential is the affinity group comprised of **Chief Academic Officers**. These key leaders have deep concern for relating holiness to campus life, particularly in relation to curricular design and programs of faculty development.

Aldersgate Press. The decision of the WHC to facilitate the formation of the Aldersgate Press was visionary. The intention of this step is reflected in the mission statement of the Aldersgate Press: "To provide a communication channel as an extension of the Wesleyan-Holiness Consortium for nurturing Christian leaders around practical themes of holiness and to encourage a new generation of writers in focusing on the growing interest in transformed Christian living through appropriating the holiness of God in lives, cultures, and structures."[16]

The Aldersgate Press has the practical vision of creating holiness literature that is accessible to the public. It is not a venue for academic scholarship. Nevertheless, its publications may serve well to help promote a pragmatic understanding of Wesleyan-Holiness and the means of living a life of holiness and righteousness. While its value is clear for persons in a diversity of ministries, it is likely to be a supportive resource to educators in higher education settings as well.

Reinventing the Heritage

We ought not to argue over whether the heritage has at least in part been lost by many and possibly most colleges and universities historically founded in the Wesleyan-Holiness tradition. The case could be made that at the heart of the educational enterprise it never fully existed. For many it began and remained on the fringe of the life of the institution as something to be covered in college chapel or in the annual revival meeting. As far as it has progressed today may be in the form of "holiness heritage week" which still is a series of chapel events.

> The real action takes place at the level of faculty and student life staff. The faculty shape the curricular experience and implement the pursuit of student outcomes on a course by course basis. They find ways to integrate faith and learning content into the syllabi and student academic experience. More importantly, the lives they live constitute their most profound form of teaching. This drives the process of Christian higher education and is key to reclaiming the heritage of holiness.

With the exception of religion classes in the beginning, Wesleyan-Holiness never made it into the curriculum broadly. With religion professors now from other traditions it is rare to encounter Wesleyan-Holiness in religion classes. Wesleyan-Holiness remains conceived as only as a crisis experience and ignored as process to be intentionally integrated across the curriculum and carried through the four years of undergraduate experience. If given attention at all, it is assigned to the campus chaplain and/or religion faculty. What remains missing is the idea of the whole university for whole person development in pursuit of holiness as the highest spiritual student outcome.

RECLAIMING THE HERITAGE

The Wesleyan-Holiness Consortium's affinity group for presidents is a laudable step. A step further would bring chief academic officers into the discussion. However, who would not agree that the real action takes place at the level of faculty and student life staff? The faculty shape the curricular experience and implement the pursuit of student outcomes on a course by course basis. They find ways to integrate faith and learning content into the syllabi and student academic experience. More importantly, the lives they live constitute their most profound form of teaching. This drives the process of Christian higher education and is key to reclaiming the heritage of holiness.

Reclaiming the heritage may be the wrong concept. Reinventing the heritage may be more accurate. Going beyond reliance on crisis experiences only and bringing educational process and crisis experience together is the way forward. Reinventing the heritage would require revisiting the way we think of higher education beyond a predominantly cognitive exercise. It would mean looking at the entire student experience of head, heart and life, as integrated education of the cognitive, affective, and behavioral, as orthodoxy, orthopathy, and orthopraxy, as theory and practice with compassion that comes from purity of heart. It would mean educational vitality, knowledge of head and heart together, integrated "knowledge and vital piety" to paraphrase John Wesley.

CHAPTER EIGHT

HOLINESS AND THE UNIVERSITY

Your fruit is growth in holiness.

Romans 6:22

All colleges and universities aspire to produce graduates of competence in their chosen fields. Institutions that offer an approach grounded in the liberal arts are no different. Regardless of the student's major in the humanities, sciences, or professions (business, nursing, fine arts) liberal arts universities and colleges strive for students to be both broadly competent in the liberal arts and more specifically in their area of study. Christian universities set the bar higher. Their intention is to produce graduates of both competence and character. Character formation is the value added nature of Christian higher education.

Competence and Character

As a president of an excellent Christian university, I would clarify to prospective students and their parents the value added nature of character and the commitment of the whole university to adding that value. I would emphasize that this is what makes the lifelong difference in deciding to study at our university over another. It was important to make clear to them that by character we mean a life after the likeness of Jesus Christ. Jesus is the prototype for every student's development. He is the ultimate example of spiritual maturity and purity of heart and life. He says clearly in scripture, "I have come that they may have life and have it more abundantly" (John 10:10).

I would emphasize the short and long-term success of our graduates who with both competence and Christ-like character had the edge over graduates from secular universities. In addition to their competence in their field, their character came through in the work place, in their professional comportment and relationships, and in their family life. Employers prefer to hire people of both competence and character. It makes sense that both are good for the enterprise.

The passion of the Christian university community is to serve in such a way that every student will progress in their development of competence and character. If our understanding of character is Christ-likeness, and if holiness is simply the likeness of Christ, the fullness of the indwelling Christ in a Christian's life, then at the heart of the added value of the university is the work of guiding students in holiness. Holiness becomes the standard for the ultimate educational vitality we desire for all student lives. Notice the idea of educational vitality. Higher education becomes more than academic competence. Higher education offers something higher. That something is vital. It is full of *vita*, life. It is more than the development of intellect, the acquisition of knowledge, memorization of facts, and the ability to reason. Higher education of the whole person brings together the intellect with the heart and is lived out through one's character. At the heart of character is the love of Christ in the student's life. The love of Christ is pure. It is selfless and self-giving. Its focus is others. It is mature and pragmatic in its impact upon others and upon the world. The essence of educational vitality and the character it occasions is found in the purity of God's love. It is seen as Christ indwelling mature Christian hearts and guiding the expressions of competence in daily living.

When it comes to the serious pursuit of competence and character in student lives, the whole university must be passionate about the whole person. By whole university, we mean everyone, not just the faculty, but every staff member from the cooks in the kitchen to the resident hall directors, the administrative assistants in the president's office to the staff that keeps the grounds and mows the lawns. It takes the total milieu of the entire university invested in the same outcome.

I remember having coffee one morning with the university's housekeeping staff. These were mostly women without a university education. They cleaned the residence halls beginning at four o'clock in the morning. I sat and listened to story after story of how students engaged them in conversations about life. Often this happened because students were still up. They hadn't gone to bed yet. In the stories it became clear that these dear staff, doing the most mundane yet necessary work, were in a privileged position of influence. They had a salutary impact on the character formation of students. To many, they were the mom away from home. They were accessible, willing to listen, and wise in the perspectives they offered. They were an effective part of the whole university for the whole person in the character development of students. They were part of the overall essence of the university.

The Essence of the University: Amazing Love

The essence of the Christian university is Jesus Christ and the essence of Christ is holy love. When Christ is at the center of the enterprise and when all faculty and staff members are centered in Christ, the love of Christ radiates out to the students and permeates their hearts and lives. The institution is a university of love.

The Beatles were one of history's most celebrated groups. Although they disbanded decades ago, their music remains popular around the world. One of their most remembered phrases from a highly popular tune is "All you need is love." While we certainly need more than love, many can resonate with the simple profundity of this phrase. In its simple, undefined claim lies its profound capacity to move the listener to a deeper meaning. We appreciate the depth of the meaning of love when we see or experience it firsthand. The more desperate, dire, or disturbing the circumstances within which love is given, the more meaningful is the understanding. Someone has rightly said that love is not so much a feeling as an action, and a series of actions, especially actions that come with a cost, with sacrifice, and with a compelling concern for the good and wellbeing of others over oneself.

Universities are not thought of as institutions of love. That is to say that they are more often places simply of transaction. The path to your degree is laid out. If you take enough courses within given guidelines, pay enough tuition, engage in multiple transactions with several professors and thereby experience enough course exposures, and trade tests and papers for grades, then you will receive your degree. While there may be some admiration involved, there isn't much room or need for love. Of all the actions involved, none could be characterized as love. In reality, to run the gauntlet of university life and succeed in getting a degree – or if you are faculty, to obtain tenure and promotions – you need a lot of things, but not love.

The university is more than the buildings and the books. The university is people. Distinctively, the Christian university is a people of love. Herein, the Christian university exists as a means of God's grace living in faith, seeking understanding, devoted to Christ, and seeking Kingdom ends. Its identity is found in Christ, and its mission is to pursue truth, make disciples, and live in obedience to the great commandment: to love the Lord with all we have within us and to love others as ourselves. Others includes especially students.

As a Christian university and therefore as a particular people, we love each other and give of ourselves to each other for the mutual well-being of each other. This is the daily bread of the university community. This is our collective, mutual calling and commission. In this way, Christ is the essence of the university. This has profound, exponential implications for all who take their place in the fellowship that the community finds in Christ and in each other. This makes the Christian university a particular people and, in contrast to so many other kinds of universities, makes us a peculiar people. They shall know us by our love.

> Higher education of the whole person brings together the intellect with the heart and is lived out through one's character. At the heart of character is the love of Christ in the student's life. The love of Christ is pure. It is selfless and self-giving. Its focus is others. It is mature and pragmatic in its impact upon others and upon the world.

Our great privilege is to be known as a university of love, of Christ's pure and holy love lived out and given away beyond each other to the world. It is peculiar. It is not normal. It is more than different. We are a peculiar people in our commitment to ends that involve love expressed through sacrifice. It is seen in our research, in scholarship that has others in mind, and in teaching with freshness and passion that moves students to love who and how we love, see what and how we see, and do what in their increasing maturity seems right to do.

This is not to say that there is no altruism, care, and concern for others at other universities. God's grace is active everywhere. It is to say that in the Christian university, the love of Christ is expressed in a calling and commitment to reaching higher ground through higher levels of discovery, learning, engagement, service and aspirations for ends that truly matter. There is a greater interest in seeing every student prosper and giving greater attention to every student's needs and potential. There is a passion for the work and a willingness to persevere toward ends that truly matter for the world's deepest challenges and most profound needs.

The Christian university, as a people of love, embraces the profound truth in the old hymn of the church, "He Giveth More Grace":

> *He giveth more grace as our burdens grow greater,*
> *He sendeth more strength as our labors increase,*
> *To added afflictions he addeth his mercy,*
> *To multiplied sorrows, he multiplies peace,*
> *His love has no limits, his grace has no measure,*
> *Hi power no boundaries known unto man,*
> *For out of his infinite riches in Jesus,*
> *He giveth, and giveth, and giveth again.*

Love gives. Love is an action. Often it involves loving the unlovable, loving with faith that love can make a tremendous difference in another's life, and loving with a love that gives glory to God. As a people of love, the Christian university loves in the likeness of Christ. Those who make up the Christian university look to serve in ways that give, and give, and give to others, drawing on the grace of God that provides strength and wisdom to make a difference.

HOLINESS AND THE UNIVERSITY

What does love look like in the Christian university? Again, the answer is that love is an action. When we observe the action of professors, we see that they take on a higher workload of teaching in order to preserve small classes that permit them to get to know their students well. This is going the extra mile and is a type of love in action. Like all things, there is a line that can be crossed in which sacrifice can spill over into exploitation of faculty by the university. Nevertheless, in small classes, faculty can be more sensitive to the potential and to the needs of their students.

Professors act in love when they take extra time to meet with students and engage them on topics with which students personally wrestle. Professors love students when they go out of their way to write lengthy responses to student papers and engage them in follow-up dialogue.

> The essence of the Christian university is Jesus Christ and the essence of Christ is holy love. When Christ is at the center of the enterprise and when all faculty and staff members are centered in Christ, the love of Christ radiates out to the students and permeates their hearts and lives. The institution is a university of love.

Professors love students when they take time to encourage the whole student, when they inquire about their family, their general well-being, and their spiritual health. Professors love students when they not only pray for them, but pray with them, when they share their own faith journey, and when they guide students in ways that strengthen their relationship with Christ. They love students when they bring them into their laboratories as lab assistants and invite them to co-author papers, when they invite them home for a home cooked meal, and join them in church on Sunday. They love students when they get to know them well enough while they are students to write strong, well-crafted letters of recommendation years after they have had them in classes. This is peculiar action for faculty. Love in the university is peculiar. It is different, and it makes all the difference. It transforms. It impacts. Love in the university is not all that is needed, but it goes a long way in the transformation of students in competence and character after the likeness of Christ.

The Essence and Likeness of Christ: Fullness of God's Holy Love

The Apostle Paul captures the essence of character in his writings to the church at Ephesus:

> I pray that out of his glorious riches he may strengthen you with power through his Spirit in your inner being, so that Christ may dwell in your hearts through faith. And I pray that you, being rooted and established in love, may have the power to grasp how wide and long and high and deep is the love of Christ, and to know this love that surpasses knowledge – that you may be filled to the measure of all the fullness of God (Ephesians 3:16-19).

God's essence, his nature, is holy love, love that is absolutely pure. It is sinless and uncontaminated. Paul is making it clear that by God's loving kindness and grace, his greatest desire is that we be like him as we see him revealed in Christ. Christ-likeness is holy love. Holiness is being filled to the measure of the fullness of God. Christ is the measure, the standard, the revelation of God's holy love.

Notice the developmental progression of Paul's prayer. First, Paul assumes that the listeners and readers are persons of faith, but that there is more that God wants to do. When you read Paul's writings carefully, you see that what is on Paul's heart and mind comes from his prayer life as God speaks to him. He prays first for strength by the power of the Holy Spirit in their inner being so that Christ may dwell in their hearts through faith. Developmentally, there is more growth and maturity possible in their faith and the opportunity for Christ to dwell in their hearts.

Dwell is a strong word. It means permanent residence, sustained presence in place day after day for the long haul. Paul prays for this because it is not the case at that time in their lives. Similarly, we pray for this in the lives of students, that they would be strengthened in their inner being so much so that Christ's residence in their hearts and lives would not be the occasional bed and breakfast, hit and run occupation, but that they would develop and mature into a dwelling relationship with Christ. Paul says it a little differently in his letter to the Colossians:

> Just as you received Christ Jesus as Lord, continue to live in him, rooted and built up in him, strengthened in the faith as you were taught (Colossians 2:6-7).

This is a developmental and educational statement. He says, "strengthened in the faith just as you were taught." The process of Christian education can facilitate such strengthening in the faith. Teaching can do that. As Christ dwells in them and takes up permanent residence (Ephesians), they are to "continue in him" (Colossians). There's the synergism, the grace and response. He dwells in us. We continue in him. Paul goes on to say, "For in Christ all the fullness of the Deity lives in bodily form, and you have been given fullness in Christ."

The fullness of God in Christ, whose essence is holy love, is holiness. God's greatest desire is that we come to know how wide and long and high and deep is the holy love of Christ. The ultimate outcome of his permanent residence is the fullness of God, his holy love, his holiness. It is God's great desire for students who are in their most formative years. They are open to being transformed. That transformation is anticipated as more than mere competence in their chosen field to merely secure a job after graduation. They are open to and looking for more.

Paul concludes his prayer for the Ephesians by referring to more, but it is a contingent more. In the context of the fullness of God and contingent on the fullness (holiness), Paul then says, "Now unto Him who is able to do immeasurably more than we ask or imagine, according to his power that is at work within us, to him be glory in the church and in Christ Jesus throughout all generations, forever and ever! Amen" (Ephesians 3:20-21).

When young people mature in their faith and come to walk in holiness and righteousness as Paul prays, continuing in Christ with Christ in permanent residence, they are filled with the fullness of God's essence, holy love. They are living the life of holiness that is God's greatest desire. They are being restored to his likeness. They are being perfected, to use John Wesley's conception of holiness as perfect love. The years that students spend in the university community are ideal for the pursuit of holiness. The university is ideally the perfect milieu for facilitating students' pursuit of the fullness of God, holiness.

> The years that students spend in the university community are ideal for the pursuit of holiness. The university is ideally the perfect milieu for facilitating students' pursuit of the fullness of God, holiness. The faculty and staff, the curriculum, all the exposures inherent in a Spirit-filled, Spirit-guided, Spirit-encountered, Christ-centered education are possible. The faculty, staff, curriculum, and exposures become the means of grace.

The faculty and staff, the curriculum, all the exposures inherent in a Spirit-filled, Spirit-guided, Spirit-encountered, Christ-centered education are possible. The faculty, staff, curriculum, and exposures become the means of grace by which real, genuine transformation takes place in the lives of students when there is a resolve to help students pursue holiness through an even higher education. Colleges and universities of Wesleyan-Holiness orientation are particularly well-suited to facilitate a higher form of higher education.

CHAPTER NINE

HOLINESS IN THE UNIVERSITY:

ESSENCE, FORM, AND IMPACT

> Put on the garments that suit God's chosen people, His own, his beloved.
>
> *Colossians 3:12*

Holiness in the university is occasioned by a greater vision of higher education than is normative. It goes beyond the paradigm that pays exclusive homage to knowledge, its formation and dissemination. It acknowledges more than the importance of academic education as transaction. It pursues a paradigm of educational vitality that takes seriously an understanding of "higher" to mean the integration of educational exposures, experiences, and encounters of the head, heart and life and the shaping of competence and character of the whole person. Before looking at the nature of holiness in the university as the holistic transformation of the whole person and the paradigms that make that possible, it is helpful to take a closer look at the essence, form, and impact of holiness in the university.

The More Excellent Way

However excellent may be the present delivery of higher education, there is a more excellent way. Holiness in the university is about engaging a university community in the redemptive, reconciling, and restorative work of the Kingdom through lives of holiness from generation to generation. It is about engaging the essence of holiness within the forms that are appropriate to the time, place and culture. Along the way, in response to God's calling to holiness, the university must be able to distinguish between form and essence and not find itself embracing forms of holiness while losing the essence of the holy God in us.[17]

In Revelation 2:2-5, we read the words of Jesus to the Church at Ephesus:

> I know your deeds, your hard work and your perseverance. I know that you cannot tolerate wicked men, that you have tested those who claim to be apostles but are not, and have found them false. You have persevered and have endured hardships for my name, and have not grown weary. Yet I hold this against you: You have forsaken your fist love.

By all outward appearances, the church at Ephesus was on the right track except for the central fact that in spite of their hard work, perseverance, and spiritual correctness, their love for God and for each other was missing. The outer form was present, but with little impact. The intrinsic reality of God's presence in the inner heart, the inward reality of God incarnate by the infilling by his very self, the indwelling nature of the Holy Spirit, the true essence of holiness was missing. The fullness of love described by the Apostle Paul to the Corinthians in the "love chapter" was the essence of holiness missing in the church at Ephesus.

We see the same problem 1,700 years later referenced in John Wesley's historical sermon delivered in the chapel at Oxford entitled "Almost a Christian." John Wesley drove the point home that the form of godliness misses the mark of an authentic Christian if it misses the essence of godliness found in purity of heart expressed in love. Throughout Wesley's life he spoke often about what it means to be "a real Christian," not merely a nominal one. This theme appeared in more than sixty sermons and spoke to this matter of holiness essence. His favorite verse seems to be Galatians 5:6: "The only thing that counts is faith expressing itself in love."

In a sermon entitled "The More Excellent Way," John Wesley shares a provocative contrast between high road and low road Christians:

> One ancient writer observed that there have been from the beginning two kinds of Christians. They (the first kind) lived an innocent life, conforming to the customs and fashions of the world in all things not sinful, doing many good works, abstaining from gross evils, and following the commandments of God. They tried to keep a clear conscience, but did not err at any particular strictness, being in most things like their neighbors. The other Christians not only kept from all appearance of evil, they were diligent in good works of every kind, and kept the commandments of God. They also worked to attain the whole mind of Christ, and to be as much like Jesus as possible. In order to do this, they walked a constant course of universal self-denial, trampling on every pleasure they were not divinely sure was pleasing to God. They took up their crosses daily, and tried unceasingly to enter in at the straight gate. They spared no pains to arrive at the summit of Christian holiness, leaving the first principles of the doctrine of Christ to go on to perfection, to

know completely the love of God that passes knowledge, and to be filled with all the fullness of God.

In regard to holiness at the heart of the university, we always have a choice. We can choose to help students walk the higher or lower path. God's calling of course is the more excellent way. While it is often the narrower path, nevertheless it leads to higher heights and deeper depths of holiness. The lower path is still a good way and on that path God can be served in a fashion, and mercy can be found at the end of life. In nearly everything we do in higher education of the whole person, however, there is a more excellent way. The overarching point is that Christian universities in pursuit of holiness choose the higher path and guide students on the more excellent way, the way of holy love.

The Form and Essence of Holiness

At the heart of any discussion of holiness in the university, then, is this matter of essence, form, and impact. To begin with, we may agree that the essence of something is its intrinsic reality, its inward nature. It is not so much its image as its "innage." The essence of something is its permanent and continuing elements that are alive and dynamic. This is in contrast to form, which may be understood to be outer appearance, image, changing and transient. In holiness the outer form is vital for it holds the inner heart from which the first love flows. The outer appearance as the form must always reflect and convey the essence, but is free to change as long as it stays true to the essence.

To speak of holiness in the university in terms of essence and form is to frame our thinking with theoretical constructs that may help to assess and critique the personal, social, and organizational/institutional nature of holiness. That's the focus of the next chapter. It helps to think of essence and form in relationship to one another, but not the same. It is always form that translates essence. Form carries essence. Form communicates essence and makes it known. One might say that form incarnates essence as in John 1:14, "The Word became flesh, and we beheld his glory as the only son of the Father, full of (essence) grace and truth."

We may describe organizational holiness when we speak of the university as essence and form in relationship to one another. The essence of the Christian university is given by God. It is the gift of himself, the very presence of God in and through the university when in obedience the church consecrates itself to God and is filled and transformed by his presence. What is then consecrated (offered up) to God is sanctified by God, Emmanuel, God with us and in us. God's nature becomes our "innage." The essence of God fills and dwells in the form of ourselves personally and as a university community.

Essence is translated into form. The relationship is always dynamic while the essence is always the same. The form may change from age to age and generation to generation. We see this in the words of the Lord through the writing of Isaiah (54:2): "Let out the curtains of your tent, don't hold back. But lengthen your cords and strengthen your stakes." This is to say, as a people with a mission of educational vitality, don't be afraid to evolve, develop, grow, mature, prosper, change in shape, capacity, size, function, symbols, and methods, but be sure to drive your stakes down deep into first things, first commitments, primary priorities. In the words of Jesus, "Seek first the Kingdom of God and his righteousness." Or in other words

> Holiness in the university is about engaging a university community in the redemptive, reconciling, and restorative work of the Kingdom through lives of holiness from generation to generation. It is about engaging the essence of holiness within the forms that are appropriate to the time, place and culture. Along the way, in response to God's calling to holiness, the university must be able to distinguish between form and essence and not find itself embracing forms of holiness while losing the essence of the holy God in us.

found in 1 Peter 1:15-16, "But just as he has called you is holy, so be holy in all you do; for it is written 'Be holy, for I am holy'" (Leviticus 11:45, 46; 19:2; 20:7).

Essence and form are interrelated. When we say we are a holy people, we acknowledge both essence and form. The essence of holiness always speaks to what God has called his people to be. It is at the heart of our existence, our identity. The forms that holiness takes are the ways and means that the essence is made known, experienced, and informed in response to the peculiar and particular contemporary exigencies and challenges of the day. In this way, where we find essence it is in some form. However, the opposite does not always hold. Where we find form that may have once carried essence, we may not necessarily find essence remaining.

Jesus spoke very clearly of this when he referenced the sad state of affairs in the inner life of the Pharisees. Today we use the stereotype of Pharisee as one who has all the form of holiness but not the substance. We characterize churches as faith communities that have all the form and function of church, but have lost the Spirit and are in reality dead, and if not dead, then dying. It raises the question as to the degree to which colleges of Wesleyan-Holiness heritage have the form of an authentic, Christ-centered, Spirit filled institution, but have lost the essence of the Spirit of God in reality.

Form does not determine essence, but rather it gives it visible shape. Essence on the other hand gives direction, impetus, and purpose to form. And it can restore form in reference to its origins in the past to assure its relevance to carry essence into the future.

HOLINESS IN THE UNIVERSITY

To speak of holiness in a person, a people, a denomination, or a university community is to speak of both essence and form at three levels: personal, social, and organizational/institutional. Much of the past holiness writings focus on the level of the personal. In my own tradition, The Salvation Army, in the writings of Commissioner Samuel Logan Brengle, General Fredrick Coutts, and many others, it is personal holiness that overwhelmingly fills the pages with *Helps to Holiness* (Brengle) regarding *The Splendor of Holiness* (Coutts). In the literature in which I am most familiar, where social holiness is discussed, it is almost completely focused on form and in particular on social ministry to the disenfranchised, needy, suffering masses on the margins of society, the "down and out" and "suffering tenth" of the community. There is an apparent disconnect between the personal holiness experience of the spirit-filled life and the social reality of the outer forms of compassion that are attributed to the inferred inner realities of holiness.

Tragically, and likely more times than we would wish to think, the outer forms may be driven by habit, normative institutionalized roles tethered to government funding and public financial support and calcified into a form of career and routine. If so, it is a rut that form has taken. The essence of holiness is missing and it lends credence to the truism that "a rut is an early grave." What is true in the Christian social services sector may be true in Christian higher education. The forms continue on, but the essence of the presence of the Spirit is no longer there. Often these forms of social service are mistakenly labeled social holiness when there is not the essence of holiness in them.

The idea of personal holiness in the aggregate of a faith community may characterize a social reality of a holy people seeking sanctification and the fullness of God. This is social holiness. This ever renewing, creative expression of a faith community is not well discussed in the holiness literature of my denomination. Attention to the ever renewing forms of a collective holiness that vibrantly carry the essence of holiness may have characterized my own faith community in earlier days, but the lament of the loss of holiness essence is too often heard in describing contemporary realities of the present day faith community. The fact that it is being discussed, noticed as diminished, and written about accordingly is an encouraging sign of renewal of the doctrine of holiness in the life of the denomination. In spite of the confusion of essence and forms of holiness, this is a good thing. These discussions include how we might better live out a sense of being a holy people. By them we raise other questions around a fuller conceptualization of social holiness, form and essence that apply also to Christian higher education and the Wesleyan-Holiness colleges and universities as educational faith communities.

Social and Organizational Forms of Holiness

One of the great contributions of John Wesley and Methodism to the world and the Kingdom of God was the means of grace constituting a social organization. The class meetings, bands, and penitent groups were forms that functioned as social/spiritual ecologies of spiritual formation and holiness. They were ordered and structured in intentional ways to permit participation in various means of grace, all within a framework of discipline and accountability. They were effective forms of social holiness within which the essence of holiness was both a personal and a social reality. At yet another level, John Wesley established an organization of Methodism as a renewal movement within the Anglican Church. The movement was open to participation by non-Anglicans and people who were highly interested, but not yet come to faith in Christ. It engaged circuit-riding lay preachers. It promoted social organizations at the local level that permitted in their forms and structures exposures to God's love along a continuum of God's justifying, sanctifying, and glorifying grace.

In recent decades many churches, denominations, colleges and universities of Wesleyan heritage largely abandoned the social forms of holiness.

HOLINESS IN THE UNIVERSITY

They let fall by the wayside the social-ecological structures and processes that were the petri dishes and hot houses in which holiness germinated and grew. These were contexts of powerful discipleship out of which saints moved into the world as salt and light, and served as redemptive, reconciling, restorative forces of unimaginable impact on the world. It was in the 1950s that class meetings had their last run in the life of many Wesleyan faith communities including colleges.

On the other hand, small group fellowship is back. It is being promoted largely in non-Wesleyan circles and only rarely related to an intentional concern for the essence of holiness. There is a disconnect between the forms that characterize Christian community life and the intentional desire be holy and promote holiness as God is holy. The small group, cell group, fellowship group innovations are back, but largely without elements that characterized Wesleyan-Holiness small group contexts. No longer do we find the discipline and accountability that held so much power and promise in the past for helping new believers grow in grace, encounter the Holy Spirit, be transformed, embrace the essence of holiness, and stay the course. Our congregations, colleges, and universities are putting in place the social forms of fellowship and Christian community life, but not necessarily in ways and by the means that effectively carry and convey the essence of holiness. If they were more reflective and intentional about seeking the essence of holiness, would not the forms that carry holiness and the impact of our colleges, universities, and church faith communities be far greater?

> In recent decades many churches, denominations, colleges and universities of Wesleyan heritage largely abandoned the social forms of holiness. They let fall by the wayside the social-ecological structures and processes that were the petri dishes and hot houses in which holiness germinated and grew. These were contexts of powerful discipleship out of which saints moved into the world as salt and light, and served as redemptive, reconciling, restorative forces of unimaginable impact on the world.

Holiness Essence and Impact

I read that at one time in the Methodist movement it was estimated that one out of thirty persons in Britain was a participant in Methodist small groups. Without a doubt, the salt and light of early Methodism with its enormous impact on society was driven by the essence of holiness in the relatively small sub-population of early Methodists. They were the leaven in the bread in the communities in which they resided in Britain, North America, Australia and beyond. These movements of the Holy Spirit expressed through social-ecological and organizational forms permeated the world with the essence of holiness. It had an impact that not only at the level of the individual, but at the level of social policy and national life.[18]

> Whatever the forms may be, the world desperately needs the impact of the people of God who are means by which the true essence of holiness becomes a great gift from God of himself. In the university, it is the faculty, staff, and other students who are means of grace that carry God's essence of holy love, given freely through graduates to a world with deep needs.

We know that the old forms that once were effective can be perpetuated without the true essence of holiness remaining. They are often old wine skins. To press the metaphor, however, new wine skins can be established and yet carry watered down wine, or sugar water. Many small fellowship groups serve as an example. Whatever the forms may be, the world desperately needs the impact of the people of God who are means by which the true essence of holiness becomes a great gift from God of himself. In the university, it is the faculty, staff, and other students who are means of grace that carry God's essence of holy love, given freely through graduates to a world with deep needs.

Any discussion of a renewal of the doctrine of holiness in colleges and universities must engage this matter of holiness form and essence, especially if Wesleyan-Holiness heritage institutions are to have an impact on the world more than can be asked for or imagined. For God so loves the world, and desires to impact the world, that he not only sent his Son but gives us the Holy Spirit as well. God makes available the essence of the God-self, holy love, to become the essence of our very selves and in the aggregate of our colleges and universities. The higher education received in Wesleyan-Holiness institutions becomes God's means of grace in the process of developing the competence and character of our graduates. In this we find God's plan to restore the world to what it was intended to be in the very beginning.

PART THREE

CHAPTER TEN

PURSUING HOLINESS IN HIGHER EDUCATION

This is the will of God, even your sanctification.

1 Thessalonians 4:3

From 1999 to 2013, it was my privilege to serve as president of two Christian institutions of higher learning, Booth University College (BUC) in Winnipeg, Manitoba (Canada) and Trinity Western University (TWU) in Langley, British Columbia (Canada). While it was true of both institutions, we were explicit to say about TWU, "The essence of TWU is Jesus Christ." To declare this was to make clear the distinctive nature of the university as a holy place. The nature of the institution and commitment of all who pursued the mission of the university was Jesus Christ. His Spirit permeated everything there to the extent that the Spirit of Jesus permeated the hearts and lives of the faculty and staff of the university. Herein, the desire was that the Holy Spirit guide and imbue the curriculum, all educational programs, and the social life of the university as a particular kind of faith community.

The essence of something is its nature, its being, its identity. In Christ, there is no difference in character between the Spirit of Jesus and the Holy Spirit. In the words of Frederick Coutts, "The Holy Spirit illuminates the mind of Christ; the life of Jesus exemplifies the work of the Spirit."[19] In the coming of the Holy Spirit at Pentecost we find all the qualities of the divine character, the possibility that all men and women may become fully Christ-like in their nature. In the words of the Apostle Peter, speaking of holiness, we may become participants in the divine nature having everything we need for life and godliness: faith, goodness, knowledge, self-control, perseverance, brotherly kindness, and love in increasing measure (2 Peter 1:3-8). The Apostle Paul says something similar in his letter to the Galatians in how we go about living in the Spirit (Galatians 5:1). We keep step with the Spirit (1:25) and take on the fruit of the Spirit: love, joy, peace, patience, kindness, goodness, faithfulness, gentleness and self-control.

Both apostles, Peter and Paul, share the attributes of Christ in these two passages of Scripture. They describe the nature or essence of holiness best understood in the light of the example of Jesus. Jesus as incarnation is nothing short of the entire disclosure of God in Christ. In Christ we see God's essence, God's holy spirit of holy love, pure love, holiness. All the qualities of the divine nature are in Christ and by the gift of the Father and Son of the Holy Spirit, the essence may take the form of humanity in our becoming fully Christ-like.

Essence: All In

When I was a young graduate student I was blessed by a great job in the summers as the program director of The Salvation Army's Camp O'Wood in the mountains outside of Tucson, Arizona. The purpose of Salvation Army camps is to help children from poor neighborhoods to 1) have a wholesome week at camp learning new skills thereby strengthening their personal sense of competence and self-esteem, and 2) grow in their character. By character was meant growing to know Jesus Christ and be like him. The development of children's competence and character in Jesus' name was the collective aspiration of the entire camp staff from the cabin counselors to the kitchen cooks.

Years later, I found myself in another great job as president of Trinity Western University. Like other Christian universities, TWU was devoted to the further development of student's competence and character. Students were developing competence in their chosen field preparing to enter the professional work world. They were also developing and deepening their walk with Christ in their character after the Lord's likeness. Much of what I had learned in the early days at camp about child development of competence and character pertained years later to the university setting. It takes everyone in the enterprise to get the job done. Takes everyone to be "all in" in being collectively the essence of Christ pursuing a common mission. All in means everyone, even those you might least expect.

> When it comes to the serious pursuit of competence and character in young people's lives, it takes the human agency of the entire enterprise being passionate about the whole person. By whole enterprise, we mean everyone, not just the faculty, but every staff member from the cooks in the kitchen to the resident hall directors, the administrative assistants in the president's office to the staff who keep the grounds and mow the lawns. By whole person we mean every aspect of human development including the spiritual, growing in grace and Christ-likeness, holiness. It takes the total milieu of the entire team invested in the same outcome.

Earlier I shared my experience of having coffee one morning with the university's housekeeping staff. Their stories were testimonies of how students would seek them out in conversations about life. These dear women were in a privileged position of influence. Accessible, willing to listen, and wise in the perspectives they offered, they had a salutary impact on the character formation of students. They were all in as an effective part of the whole university for the whole person. They were a special part of the overall essence of the university as the tangible love of Christ. The same could be said about the maintenance staff, the bookstore staff, and the other areas of the university who were all in.

When it comes to the serious pursuit of competence and character in young people's lives, it takes the human agency of the entire enterprise being passionate about the whole person. By whole enterprise, we mean everyone, not just the faculty, but every staff member from the cooks in the kitchen to the resident hall directors, the administrative assistants in the president's office to the staff who keep the grounds and mow the lawns. By whole person we mean every aspect of human development including the spiritual, growing in grace and Christ-likeness, holiness. It takes the total milieu of the entire team invested in the same outcome.

God is an "all in" God. He did not hold back his great gift of salvation on the cross, nor his subsequent gift of himself as the Holy Spirit. He is "all in" for the world. In Christian higher education, why settle for something less. When Christ says, "Follow me," it's a call for us to also be "all in" in essence so that the essence of the university truly is Jesus Christ. When that is a reality, the university is a holy place and the work of the university as a particular faith community is sacramental.

Pursuing Transformation

Form carries essence. It always has, but the form often changes over time. In Christian higher education the form has undergone remarkable changes. Often the essence is lost and yet the forms continue even for centuries. The four waves of higher education speak directly to this reality. You recall the early form of the ancient academies followed by monasteries. These transformed into two kinds of institutions, monasteries for the education of clergy and cathedral schools for the laity. Over time the cathedral schools became the early forms of the Christian university (Bologna, Salamanca, Paris, Oxford).

The early European universities set the pattern for the New World colonial universities, first in Latin America and then in the North American colonies. The transformation of Harvard College from a thoroughly Christian institution to a thoroughly secular university set the pattern for hundreds of Christian colleges and universities over a period of a few hundred years to the present day. Over time the forms continued, while the essence dissipated. What remains is a remnant of Christian colleges and universities, some with a historical Wesleyan commitment to holiness of heart and life. Nevertheless, the institutions in the remnant find themselves under siege from a host of pressures toward secularism and struggling to hold on to the essence of holiness at the heart of the enterprise.

The Promise of Transformation

All universities and colleges today promise transformation. It is the latest buzz in marketing higher education. Like all universities, transformation is the promise Christian institutions also make to prospective students and their parents. After four years of higher education the promise is that the student will be a different person. The exposures they experience will facilitate a transformative experience and they will be changed. In the secular universities, the promise is an academic one meaning preparation to enter the professional field of the student's choice and possibly become a solid citizen in one's community. In Christian higher education, the promise is the same and more. Students will ideally grow in a more holistic way, including the transformation to spiritual maturity, strengthened in their faith, and better prepared to live in ways pleasing to God. For many parents it may be enough that their son or daughter not lose faith along the way.

For many graduates of Christian colleges and universities, the promise of transformation reflects a ratio of the two types of Christians John Wesley describes. In the previous chapter, I shared a quote from a sermon by John Wesley entitled "The More Excellent Way." You will remember John Wesley presented a provocative contrast between high road and low road Christians.

As I noted earlier, we can choose to walk either path. God's calling of course is the more excellent way. While it is often the narrower path, nevertheless it leads to higher heights and deeper depths of holiness. The lower path is still a good way and on that path God can be served in a fashion. Mercy can be found at the end of life. Still, we are faced with this biblical assertion: "Without holiness no one will see God" (Hebrews 12:14). In nearly everything we do, there is a more excellent way.

Every Christian college and university graduates a ratio of high and low path students. Since institutions do not have explicit student outcomes related to high path holiness nor assessments of such, it is impossible to know an institution's ratio. The idea of a ratio is a hypothetical construct to make a point. It may be fair to say it is rare that an institution has an impulse to graduate as many high path students as possible and invests in a self-assessment accordingly.

So, how do Christian colleges and universities facilitate the higher path for a greater number of students? How can a powerful university promote the kind of holistic transformation of students so that, following graduation, they keep going on the more excellent way? This is a question of balancing both competence and character.

What faculty member does not aspire the very best for her or his students? We take pride in seeing our students achieve entrance into prestigious medical schools, law schools, and doctoral programs. We rejoice when they are hired as teachers in local school systems, as engineers, architects, or in other professions. We work hard to facilitate their competence in chosen fields and to see them move on to become the very best in their area of interest. The passion for promoting competence must be balanced with a passion for the transformation of character, of inner and outer holiness. It takes the whole university to keep the promise to transform the whole person into the likeness of Christ.

The *Milieu* of Transformation

Colleges and universities are *milieus* of transformation. Another way to say this is that they are social contexts in which people potentially thrive and flourish depending on what the university provides. In the typical university or college, a student is exposed to opportunities for intellectual development, but not much in the way of spiritual growth and maturity, and some exposures can also be toxic. Christian colleges and universities hold the promise of helping student flourish completely, thrive holistically in body, mind, spirit and soul depending on the essence of the university and its intention to be holistic. For the student, choosing any college or university is a choice of immersion. It is a decision to be immersed in a social/spiritual ecology of grace and opportunity and/or in a *milieu* which can be rife with toxicity. Both contexts can promote transformation. The question is what kind of transformation is most desirable?

> The acquaintance process may be the most powerful, influential paradigm operating on a college or university campus in that it incorporates all the characteristics of the other paradigms and carries the comprehensive educational (not just academic) experience along the way.

When the Apostle Paul uses the phrase "grow in grace," we recognize that there is an ecology of grace and holiness. The little word "in" contextualizes holiness to suggest an ecological metaphor. Ecology deals with relationships between organisms and their environment. The key to thinking ecologically is to remember that every living thing is immersed in a context or environment. Both the organism and the environment has specific characteristics.

Just as there are biological ecologies, so there are social-spiritual contexts where people are immersed in the environment. The college and university are such contexts. The Christian college and university are social-spiritual ecologies with specific characteristics. As a tadpole may find itself in a nutrient-balanced ecology of the bulrushes of a pristine mountain stream, so may a student be immersed in a social-spiritual setting of the university filled with opportunities, exposures, and encounters that promote growth and development socially, physically, intellectually, and spiritually. Christian higher education settings can be powerful contexts. There students may be immersed in a qualitatively different form of higher education. These are settings where the essence of Jesus Christ is real, and where the whole institution and all who serve there fulfill the institution's mission.

> God uses others (home, family, professors, coaches, staff members, administrators) to mediate his grace to students and all who step foot on the holy ground of a college or university that is "all in" in the mission and ministry of a whole university that serves the whole person. And God honors and sustains the college and university that pursues holiness in higher education in a social-spiritual ecology of holiness.

However, ecologies including colleges and universities can be weak and deficient in what they provide. If a university is primarily providing higher education as a transaction with emphasis on academic competence, it is likely deficient and weak in addressing the needs and potential of the whole person. Even worse, like a stream polluted by industrial waste, colleges and universities can be toxic.

There was a time when the Cuyahoga River, flowing into Lake Erie at Cleveland, carried the most toxic sludge of industrial pollutants imaginable. Nothing lived in its putrid, foul waters. It was so bad that in the summer of 1969 the river caught fire from a cigarette thrown off the back of a freighter. It is a testimony to the idea of restoration that today the river is restored to its earlier, healthy state.

Toxic pollution of industry was arrested and the river over several years was restored.

Like the Cuyahoga River, some university and college settings are so toxic they are contexts of spiritual destruction where faith dissipates and is even destroyed. This is not to say that students cannot spiritually survive toxic college and university environments. The odds favor students who are strong in their faith and daily walk. But for some students, especially those who are not strong, some settings are high risk for Christian spiritual mortality.

Here's why: (1) university education is built mostly on high status, high influence persons called faculty of whom very few (17% at best) are Christians. The overwhelming number of faculty on most universities and colleges are either agnostic or committed atheists. A critical mass of faculty is boldly hostile to Christianity and to students who are Christians. (2) The same may be said for the percentage of student peers at the university. The normative life style on most campuses is minimally distracting and more often it is outright toxic. (3) University and college campus settings are largely void of opportunities to continue the Christian journey, including worship, corporate prayer, Bible study, fellowship, and the integration of faith with the subjects that students are learning. (4) A Christian worldview to contextualize the university experience is not available.

Too often the result over a four-year bachelor degree experience is the total dissipation of faith. A student may come from a very healthy family milieu. His/her parents may have done everything right in providing a spiritually healthy family setting for growing strong children, but university and college settings can be powerful alternative contexts that can undo all the good that was accomplished in the home. Students may remain nice people, good citizens, and persons of ethics and charity, but faith in Christ dissipates and their faith journey with Christ goes in the other direction.

The option to this rather familiar and sad picture is Christian higher education. Ideally, such settings offer an enormous value added alternative.

Students in Christian universities and colleges are immersed in contexts where the means of grace are available. Faith is integrated with learning. Professors are spiritually supportive. The Christian worldview is normative and spiritual maturity is an intentional student outcome of the institution. In such settings, the exposures and encounters give students a chance to spiritually flourish into Christ-likeness. This is the ideal scenario one would hope for in every Christian college and university.

Too often though even Christian colleges and universities are not contexts of optimal holistic development. The impact of too many are mitigated compromise occasioned by financial struggle, accreditation pressures, local and state regulations, and faculty and staff who are not "all in." They are further burdened by an orientation to the mission that has all the traditional forms of higher education, but lost the educational vitality of the Spirit that helps students find the spiritual high road. The institution that produces low road graduates is no longer characterized by the pervasive essence of Christ in the ecological balance of the institution.

If indeed the tendency of fire is to go out, the fire, passion, and commitment to Jesus Christ as the essence of the university or college can dissipate. Sometimes what is left are only embers that evoke nostalgia for earlier days. The institution's fidelity to the promise of transformation is only partially realized. The potential for sending out godly Christian leaders of competence and Christ-like character into the world is compromised by an ecology of transformation that is too weak to fully deliver on the promise of real transformation.

Boundless Salvation

Transformation takes place when individuals are immersed in a social-spiritual context, an ecology of grace. Such an ecology we find in the celebration of God's love and grace in the words of a song by William Booth, "O boundless salvation, deep ocean of love." Booth uses an ecological metaphor of immersion to speak of God's measureless love. It is powerful imagery that encompasses all the stages of the Christian life as it progresses from beginning to end. As we stand on the beach, the living waters of God's grace begin to wash up over our feet. We are then confronted with the decision whether to walk deeper into his love, accepting his justifying grace as Savior and Lord, or to retreat the other way.

There is more to the Christian life than seeking to remain ankle-deep or even waist deep. There is a boundless salvation and a deep ocean of God's love. There is the process of wading deeper and deeper through reading and meditating upon his Word, by means of a devotional prayer life, and through fellowship with other believers. There is a crisis commitment of the whole person (consecration) as one plunges beneath the water, experiencing sanctifying grace as the fullness of God's Holy Spirit in one's life. And there is the joy of swimming, diving, snorkeling, windsurfing, and sailing in the deep ocean of God's love, experiencing his glorifying grace.

Booth's metaphor unpacks John Wesley's continuum of grace, the *via salutis*. In seven verses he covers the ground from coming to faith and justification, through the struggle of temptation and sin, to sanctifying grace, and finally in verse seven the maturity of a life of glorifying grace. His song gives an image of God's boundless, never ending love. He portrays God's love like an ocean available to be experienced by any and all. It is a full salvation from sin to holiness. Booth helps us understand several things about the immersion in the ecology of holiness. First, God desires that we develop and progress. We need not stay on the beach or just put our foot in the water from time to time. There's more. We can move forward in our relationship with Christ, and if we do he does a deepening work. Often the work is done in a social and spiritual context where others are present, involved, and engaged by God in human agency as means of grace and therefore always in the context of God's presence.

Second, God's love and presence is always prevenient. At every stage and every level of growth and development, his love goes before us. Wave upon wave in ever-flowing abundance, God's love makes possible the process and progress of moving us into maturity, growing our capacity to live in the deeper waters of God's love.

Third, to mix metaphors, as we progress our diet changes. We no longer depend on the milk of babes. God provides an appropriate environment through the means of grace that promotes our growth and well-being, often through the love of others. The means of grace includes good teaching, fellowship, breaking of bread, corporate worship, the sacraments, reading, hearing, and meditating on the Word of God, giving and hearing testimonies of God's love, confessing and repenting of sin, fasting, participating in acts of mercy and service to others, artistic expressions in art and music, moral literature, wholesome activities of small group accountability, fellowship, and more.

A college or university setting that is nutrient appropriate in the means of grace can be an ecology of grace and holiness. It can promote the progressive immersion of students into a growing relationship with Christ, a relationship of progressive acquaintance, friendship, and intimacy with Jesus by the work of the Holy Spirit in and through the human agency of faculty, staff, and students. It is not difficult to see how a spiritual ecology of grace and holiness in a college or university experience can take many forms that carry the essence of God's presence and character. And it is not difficult to see how the forms that carry the essence are relational and social.

Samuel Logan Brengle was often heard to echo John Wesley in saying that there is no holiness in the Christian life outside of social holiness. God uses others (home, family, professors, coaches, staff members, administrators) to mediate his grace to students and all who step foot on the holy ground of a college or university that is "all in" in the mission and ministry of a whole university that serves the whole person. And God honors and sustains the college and university that pursues holiness in higher education in a social-spiritual ecology of holiness.

CHAPTER ELEVEN

PARADIGMS OF ENGAGEMENT

I have not yet reached perfection, but I press on.

Philippians 3:12

There is a high road and a low road of spiritual formation and maturity. A worthwhile study of Christian university graduates would be to capture an understanding of the ratio of high to low road graduates at the time of graduation and subsequently in a prospective study design going forward well into adulthood. The study would be grounded in differentiating the nature of the college or university experience of engagement in particular types of social/spiritual ecologies and the paradigms of engagement that characterized those institutions.

How many schools are functioning at a high level of engagement as social/spiritual contexts promoting high road graduates? Another way to say this is to ask if the ratio of high road to low road alumni is stacked in favor of low road, spiritually underdeveloped Christians with little interest in pursuing a life of holiness. One would hope that all Christian colleges and universities would commit to a favorable ratio of producing high road graduates of competence and character after the likeness of Christ, filled with the fullness of God, holiness.

Four Paradigms of Engagement

Colleges and universities best engage students as social/spiritual ecologies of educational vitality for the whole person around four particular paradigms of engagement:

1. **Small Behavior Settings.** One lesson we learned from John Wesley, well before environmental psychologists discovered it, is the power of small groups. Small groups are by far more engaging than large ones. They are small behavior settings that offer a higher level of participation for each member. They occasion a higher level of familiarity and comfort with the others in the group and a higher degree of trust. This is in large part why John Wesley's small group class meetings were so effective. In those small behavior settings within the structure of the rules for the groups, every person had an opportunity to share, to be heard, to listen, and to grow with the support of the others. Wesley's class meetings were healthy. They were small enough to be dynamic and interactive for everyone in the group. In this engaging context, class meetings brokered spiritual nutrients of the means of grace including Scripture, prayer, testimonies, confessions and repentance, reports of service in response to needs. No one was left out of the conversation. No one was ignored. Everyone was supported by and held accountable for spiritual progress by everyone else in the group.

Colleges and universities differ in the degree to which they are designed and organized to promote small, intimate behavior settings. They differ in class sizes, teaching styles, and the ways social and spiritual activities are promoted and offered. Several years ago, I invited a consulting firm to campus to help us think through a new campus plan for the future. This particular consultant group worked on campus planning for over one hundred major universities and were Christians in their personal faith commitments.

A decade before, a prior administration did the same and asked their consultants what the university might look like if it were to grow its enrollment by fifty percent. I had a different question. I asked our consultants what the university might look like if it were to be a dynamic, interactive campus committed to developing Christ-like graduates. They spent a year with faculty, staff, students, alumni, donors, and others in small group discussions about the key question. They got under our skin and looked into our hearts and minds. They brought local architects, landscaping professionals, and others to campus as part of the consultation process. Their work resulted in five guiding principles with detailed examples.

One of the guiding principles was to build into the university setting many, many places where small groups could gather, formally and informally, within campus structures and outside in landscaping. They gave examples not only in the residence halls, but everywhere: outside of faculty offices, in the library, along the walkways, in the lobbies of every building, in the bookstore, throughout the physical activities center, and so on. They understood that the physical setting could be designed to promote a natural proliferation of dynamic, small behavior settings for

> How many schools are functioning at a high level of engagement as social/spiritual contexts promoting high road graduates? Is the ratio of alumni is stacked in favor of low road, spiritually underdeveloped Christians with little interest in pursuing a life of holiness? One would hope that all Christian colleges and universities would commit to a favorable ratio of producing high road graduates of competence and character after the likeness of Christ, filled with the fullness of God, holiness.

social/spiritual interaction and engagement. Christian college and university campuses can be designed and renovated to increase the potential of small behavior settings for the purpose of engagement in small groups.

2. Location, Location, Location. These are the three most important words in the area of real estate sales. Ask any real estate sales person. They will agree. Location highly determines the price of a home or office setting. That's why homes in Hawaii, San Francisco, Vancouver, Toronto, Manhattan, Boston, or London cost so much. The advantages of some locations far outweigh the advantages of others. The exposures and probability of key encounters for social and economic activities are far greater depending on the location.

The same may be said for spiritual location. For students and faculty in Christian colleges and universities, congratulations may be offered for choosing a Christian location for educational engagement. The emphasis here is on educational and not just academic engagement, educational meaning a context of the whole college or university for the whole person. Locating in a Christian behavior setting is good start. Locating in a Christian college or university with an abundance of small, formal and informal behavior settings is even better. Locating in such a setting is best where the university is intentionally committed to powerful, whole person engagements that include exposures to means of grace and spiritual disciplines leading to encounters with Christ.

Location can determine the degree of progress along a high road of holiness. Frederick Coutts once said, "The experience of Christian holiness may be defined as one in which the whole person is redirected towards the highest spiritual end—that is, likeness to Christ, and in this he or she is granted the continual help of the Holy Spirit." The chances of this happening are highly impacted by spiritual location.

Depending on the institutional location and its character, essence and commitment, the students, and all who make up the educational community, will find themselves located in the holy presence of God the Father, Jesus the Son, Lord, and Savior, and the Holy Spirit. The sustained location of every student increasingly near to the heart of God is something the college or university can and must do if it is to shift the ratio of low to high road graduates. Location for spiritual formation and purity of heart holiness is paramount. Location, that is proximity and frequency of contact of the students with God, is the means by which students may become increasingly acquainted with God. It is the way they become increasingly intimate with God and are shaped into the likeness of Christ.

The same, of course, may be said for faculty, staff, and the college or university president. It is a journey. The college years are times for student grounding, momentum, and launching into a life of fidelity and growth in grace. In relation to Christ, spiritual formation may be facilitated by the university through the acquaintance process.

3. The Acquaintance Process. One of the most powerful paradigms of engagement is the acquaintance process. Most students enter college or university not knowing anyone. Most graduate with an abundance of friends and acquaintances. They continue to hold in esteem their favorite professors and staff. Life long memories of a highly relational, educational experience prevail. Whether or not students were to some degree shy or outgoing, they were immersed in a dynamic, interactive social/spiritual context where the acquaintance process led to powerful relationships. In some settings, the exposures and encounters along the way were not all positive. Some were even toxic. Regardless, the process followed steps and engaged principles that were understandable and unfolded as follows:

1. Don't know anything about the other. Those who become good friends and favorite professors are completely unknown when the student arrives on campus.

2. Know something about him/her. By rumor or direct interactive experience, the student begins to know about the other.

3. Know him/her. Through proximity and frequency of contact there is engagement with accompanying exposures and encounters. Small behavior settings increase the opportunities for engagement. Location of proximity makes possible frequent opportunities to get to know the other.

4. Know them well and seek them out for increased opportunities for engagement. Location, proximity, and contact are initiated more frequently leading to a stronger acquaintance, friendship, and special connection. A common history is developed and shared values are developed and/or discovered.

5. Interpersonal intimacy and deep appreciation (understanding) is achieved.

   The acquaintance process may be the most powerful, influential paradigm operating on a college or university campus in that it incorporates all the characteristics of the other paradigms and carries the comprehensive educational (not just academic) experience along the way.

This is where holiness comes into play. It is the acquaintance process and the ways in which the college or university occasions the nature of the process and its content that determines a student's spiritual formation and progress toward Christ-likeness. Many students come with some knowledge about God and even about Christ. They may come from good Christian families, churches, and youth groups. My experience over the years is that increasingly many students arrive at the university biblically illiterate and having no personal relationship with Christ. They don't really know the gospel narrative. Worship is a social, community exercise with sincerity and some degree of emotion, but it remains an activity quite unrelated to other areas of a student's life (social, cognitive, physical).

In short, many students come from good Christian backgrounds, are fragmented rather than integrated in who they are as persons, and are in the earliest stages of an acquaintance with God. They know about him, but don't really know him or know him well. The task at hand is one of institutional commitment to students who are often "babes in Christ," to take them beyond competence by helping them develop character at the highest level by becoming greatly acquainted with Christ.

It is a challenge and a privilege to facilitate the acquaintance process for students with Christ on the college or university campus. The institution that is "all in" and permeates with the essence of Jesus Christ is positioned for the task. The commitment to small behavior settings and the promotion of proximity to Christ sets the stage for their engagement. It starts with faculty being genuine and transparent about their own faith position and journey with Christ. This is a matter of faculty and staff letting their light shine in such a way that students see their good works, infer their good heads and hearts, and by the quality of their life in Christ give glory to God.

> A serious essential in moving the institution in a direction of fidelity to its mission is the faculty. Every faculty member appointed moves the institution forward or backward. It is like one's faith journey. There is no such thing as stasis.

My son is now in his thirties, but when he was twelve or thirteen years of age I noticed him wearing a WWJD rubber bracelet. You may remember that WJJD meant "What would Jesus do?" At that time he seemed troubled over something and I asked him, "What would Jesus do about it?" His response surprised me. He said, "Dad, WWJD doesn't work for me. But WWAMD does work. What would Aunt Marty do?" Aunt Marty was

Marilyn, a very close friend of the family who off and on during that period would live with us for a few weeks while working on her masters degree at the college nearby. Her life and her love to our son was special. He watched her and admired her. He trusted her and in her he could see Jesus. If I asked him to describe Jesus at the time, I believe he would have given an accurate description of Aunt Mary.

> The acquaintance process may be the most powerful, influential paradigm operating on a college or university campus. This is where holiness comes into play. It is the acquaintance process and the ways in which the college or university occasions the nature of the process and its content that determines a student's spiritual formation and progress toward Christ-likeness.

This is what happens with students who know a little about Christ. They start to know more by watching the faculty and staff. As they get to know them, they get to know Christ. As they let their light shine, the glorious testimony of their Christ-like life shines through to the glory of God. The students are on their way to becoming better acquainted with and intimate with God. Location comes into play here. By being in the presence of faculty and staff who live in the presence of God students spiritually locate God's presence as well. Faculty and staff become an effective means of grace by which God reveals his identity to students and connects with them in the spiritual acquaintance process.

4. Exposures, Reflection, Dialogue. The first three paradigms discussed so far are Small Behavior Settings, Location, and The Acquaintance Process. The fourth paradigm stands in great contrast to the student experience in the large behavior settings of large universities that have large classes sometimes of a few hundred each. Faculty there are distant and educationally remote. The acquaintance process is restrained by lack of opportunity for proximity and contact. The individual is easily lost in the large numbers of other students. Engagement is not impossible, but

PARADIGMS OF ENGAGEMENT

difficult. In large institutions with large classes the educational paradigm is restricted to exposure, test, forget. There students are exposed to the text and lecture and take tests that are largely short answers (true-false, multiple choice, short paragraph essay). It is a highly disengaged exercise. Large behavior settings constrain the interpersonal opportunities of engagement between student and professors. Small behavior settings liberate those opportunities.

In contrast, small behavior settings offer a radically different opportunity. The classes are small, not more than twenty students. Professors are close and responsive. The paradigm is exposure (text, lecture, and outside class conversations), reflection, and dialogue. Reflection is paramount. Students write in every class for the four years of undergraduate study. Writing forces reflection. Faculty have time with small classes to write back and respond to student thought. In short, faculty interact with and encounter the thinking of the students. Reflection and faculty response set the stage for dialogue about the topic. Over the four years of exposure and encounter facilitated by writing, response and dialogue, students develop their skills of integrating and internalizing their studies over the time and content of their education. This is an ideal paradigm for promoting the process of sanctifying grace, growing by grace in heart and life.

Through exposure, reflection, and dialogue with integration and internalization, students come to own their educations. It becomes a part of them. The student experience is especially rich when the college or university gives students the freedom to integrate their faith with their learning, to write about how faith informs their learning and learning informs their faith. In this richer educational context, one may see how the writing and discussion of faith issues along the journey can promote spiritual formation and the acquaintance process. The writing of a first year, first semester student will look and sound different from the last semester, fourth-year student. The faculty will pose different questions at the beginning in contrast to the end of the students' studies. They will respond differently with deeper insights and wisdom as students develop their own personal relationship with Christ and mature in their understanding of who they are and who God in Christ is also.

A Nutrient Rich Spiritual Ecology: Means of Grace

The value added nature of Christian colleges and universities is their potential for engaging students and helping them grow over time in (not into) the likeness of Christ. It is occasioned by intentional exposures to God's grace and inevitable encounters with God. The context occasions proximity and contact with Christ through exposures to Scripture, prayer, fellowship, community worship, small group and personal discussions all naturally engaging students in the essence of the institution through the human agency of faculty, staff, and other students.

The forms of the academic experience are similar in many ways to all colleges and universities, but radically different in the educational experience. In the Christian setting, education of the whole person is pursued. A nutrient rich spiritual ecology engaging multiple means of God's grace helps students come to a saving knowledge of God in Christ. In and through the means of grace the Holy Spirit, the Spirit of Truth, the Counselor guides students to experience salvation from sin and also salvation to holiness and Christ-likeness. The value added nature of salvation for some students may include a low road salvation experience, but for many others there is the possibility of a high road, full salvation experience.

While the human agency of faculty and staff may be the most powerful means by which God works in the acquaintance process, there are other means characteristic of a university or college that promote student progress towards the highest spiritual ends. They serve as indicators of the institution's commitment to the essence of the institution being the Spirit of Christ. These include such investments as library holdings, visiting lecture series related to holiness, supplemental readings to key courses, and prospective institutional research that assesses student outcomes including spiritual maturity and identity of graduates with an identity of holiness.

The library is a straightforward indicator of commitment. What's on the shelves of the library? Has the college or university been investing in the very best literature on holiness? Are the classic writers in the Wesleyan-Holiness tradition found in the library collection? Does the library contain contemporary Wesleyan-Holiness authors? Regarding supplemental reading in key courses, what's on the shelves of the college or university book store? What does the book store offer in reading outside of course syllabi? Does the institution promote endowed lecture series that promote a Wesleyan-Holiness message, and do visiting lecturers fit the intent of the lecture series?

Finally, does the institution include the matter of spiritual maturity and identity regarding holiness in its institutional research on student outcomes? This presupposes that holiness is a desired student outcome among all educational student outcomes valued by the college or university. It also presumes a clear definition of holiness and indicators from which holiness can be inferred.

These are but a few ways in which a nutrient rich spiritual ecology may be supported toward the desired outcome of serving the needs of the whole person. Without a doubt there are other supportive ways to direct students toward the highest spiritual end of likeness to Christ and a life of continuing, growing intimacy with God through the Holy Spirit. Paradigms of engagement in the promotion of holiness outcomes for students must be largely in place to carry the institution's intent. The forms must be flexible, but what is paramount in importance is the college or university's abiding resolve to promote the essence of holiness, in both process and crisis, through the abundant means of grace that are possible in the social/spiritual context of the educational faith community.

Empowered Discipleship

When the Christian college or university promotes holiness as an ultimate student outcome, it becomes a powerful instrument of discipleship. By balancing a curriculum of the head, heart, and life with a focus on students becoming increasing like Christ, the college and university community empowers and gives momentum to a lifelong journey of discipleship. The high way of holiness in head and heart becomes the familiar way of Christian living for the graduate. The mind and heart of Christ become the new normal that guides lifelong and life-longing discipleship.

Throughout the student's educational experience the holiness oriented institution facilitates the coming together of the head (cognitive, intellect), heart (affective, compassion), and Christian life (active, behavioral). Many and often most students arrive at the university with these three domains fragmented and disconnected. The Christian university brings them increasingly together (integrated/blended). Where the three domains overlap is the heart of discipleship, the increasing likeness of Christ, and the desire to follow Christ in obedience and faithfulness. The overlap reflects the increasing faith and love wherein Wesley's favorite verse, Galatians 5:6, becomes a reality: "The only thing that counts is faith expressing itself through love." Higher education is higher, a new normal, when it is truly one of discipleship, growing in grace, and growing in the love and likeness of Jesus Christ by the work of the Holy Spirit in and through them.

Graphically, the student's ideal discipleship journey through his/her college or university years looks like this:

PARADIGMS OF ENGAGEMENT

UPON ARRIVAL ON CAMPUS

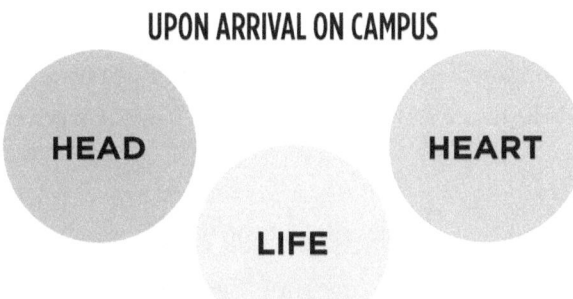

For most students the three areas of their lives are compartmentalized and disconnected. Some things they've learned remain disconnected with little impact on how they feel or how they live. Faith is a cognitive ascent to propositions. The heart is moved by many things and often paradoxically by things that are in opposition to each other. Life is lived unguided by the prudence of head and heart working together. There is little integration of the three. Nevertheless, there is the possibility of a learning experience over time that helps bring the three together and leads to a transformation of the spirit by the Spirit.

This is the task of Christian higher education in the Wesleyan-Holiness way.

BY THE END OF YEAR ONE

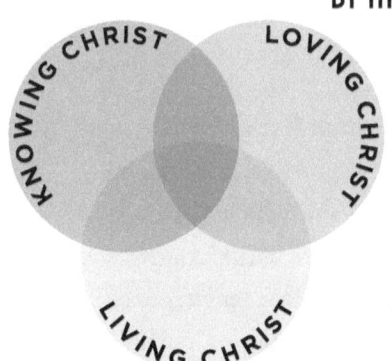

By the end of the first year, the student is progressing at bringing head, heart, and living (orthodoxy, orthopathy, orthopraxy; intellect, affect, and behavior) together in an integrated, blended manner at the center of which is Christ. This happens when the university environment is rich in exposures to the means of grace and when the university's paradigms of engagement are active. When the three begin to come together, the essence of discipleship is the student experience.

BY THE END OF FOUR YEARS

By the time the student graduates with his/her degree, significant progress of discipleship has occurred. The overlapping center of head, heart and daily living makes possible a person increasingly after the likeness of Christ, living for and serving Christ with a head (mind of Christ) and pure heart, with a capacity to be filled with the fullness of God (holiness). The overlap in a mature disciple makes it possible for him/her to continue with the help of the Holy Spirit to go forward with an increasing love for and likeness to Christ. It makes possible going forward in Christ, rooted and established in love with the power of all the saints to grasp how wide, and long and high and deep is the love of Christ, and to manifest a love that surpasses knowledge, a knowledge of the heart and brings together head and heart to guide life in the Spirit.

EVENTUALLY

Christian higher education in the Wesleyan-Holiness way makes possible a lifelong journey with Christ during which the overlapping of head, heart, and living continue in the Spirit. The overlapping center grows as the head and heart grow, making possible an increased filling of the fullness of God. The whole university committed to the whole development of the whole student provides the promise, potential, and momentum for the graduate to be blessed by a lifetime of obedience to God's direction and growth in grace, love, and likeness to Christ. The ultimate student outcome is holiness in which Christ is perfecting, completing, and restoring the student over their life time to the *Imago Dei*.

CHAPTER TWELVE

SERIOUS ESSENTIALS

What does the Lord require of thee but to do justly, love mercy, and walk humbly with your God.

Micah 6:8

If a college or university in the Wesleyan-Holiness tradition is serious about student outcomes of character in the likeness of Christ, it will embrace and be faithful to five essentials. These include faculty hiring, dean and department chair selection, board support, commitment to a strong liberal arts core, and the promotion of educational vitality through the comprehensive integration of academic and student life programs, and a community covenant.

Faculty-Mission Fit

Twenty-five years ago, I shifted from my comfortable full professorship with tenure in a large public university to the trials and tribulations of college administration as the chief academic officer of a Christian college. The president who hired me was "long in the tooth." He had accrued a great deal of experience over many years as Dean of the Faculty (now referred to as the Provost or VP for academic affairs) and as president. He had a special ability to articulate very simple truths. One day he said to me, "The legacy of a president is the board he leaves behind, but the legacy of a chief academic officer is the faculty." In elaborating he said, "The faculty will outlast your tenure and inevitably determine the direction of the institution."

> Every department is looking for its place in the sun to market their programs and majors. The result is a core curriculum that is too big and loaded with too many courses. When this happens, the core by default serves to introduce undecided students to their major field of study and fails to serve the greater mission of the institution.

A serious essential in moving the institution in a direction of fidelity to its mission is the faculty. Every faculty member appointed moves the institution forward or backward. It is like one's faith journey. There is no such thing as stasis. Like one's personal faith, the institution is a living, dynamic, interactive reality because it is made up of people of faith and commitment. Every faculty member hired is a critical part of the fabric of faith of the institution. This begs the question of how resolved the leadership of the institution is to search for and aggressively recruit faculty with a strong fit with the values and mission of the institution. Recruitment must be done with student outcomes in mind. This is not only desirable. It is essential. To do otherwise is to risk weakening the capacity of the university to be faithful to first things.

Questions for a university seeking fidelity to its Wesleyan-Holiness heritage include: Upon hiring do faculty testify to their own personal holiness experience? Do they understand the basic idea of full salvation and sanctification? Do they view themselves being perfected in their spiritual journey?

SERIOUS ESSENTIALS

Mid-level Leadership

The real action in filling a particular faculty position is not with the president and Provost. However, they set the stage for success depending on who they appoint to the mid-level leadership positions of dean and department chair. Deans recommend the appointment of department chairs and work on a daily basis with them. Together they shape the position announcements, advertise, and appoint a search committee for each position hired. The dean and department chairs control and influence the quality of the file of prospective candidates. They are particularly influential in being in accord with the search committee regarding the candidates invited for an interview. To be highly valued is the dean and department chair's involvement in the campus visit of finalists and their discernment. They must not only discern the candidates' academic capacity and strength, but also their character, personal spiritual commitment, and their fit with the spiritual aspirations of the institution. This is something that should not be solely the duty of the Provost or President.

One of my great frustrations as president was being in a system where the search committees, department chairs, deans, and provost only looked at the academic prowess of candidates. At best, they would discern if the candidate was a regular church attender. As president, I was left to explore the depths of their spiritual journey, the extent to which they presently had a live, active, engaged faith, and their fit spiritually with the mission of the university. With all the strengths of that particular institution, this was its Achilles heel and its soft-spot of vulnerability. I pressed the issue over time. It did improve. It never was fully resolved to my satisfaction. Faith and fidelity to mission issues are best superintended by the deans, department chairpersons, and search committees as well as the provost and the president. It signals to the candidate the ethos and essence of the institution, holiness, Christ in us.

Asking the right questions is the key to the right recruitment of faculty and academic leadership. Questions in the process of appointing mid-level leadership include: Do their lives correspond well to the priorities of the university in the pursuit of holiness as a desirable student outcome? Do they facilitate a context where the whole university serves as a social/spiritual milieu (ecology) of holiness? Do they promote a strong fit in faculty hiring development with a holiness ethos and institutional aspirations? Are they all in?

Board Support

My friend, a wise president back in the nineties, was mostly right when he said that the legacy of the president is the board of trustees, governors, or directors. The president often is in a position to recommend to the board those prospective board members whose values and interest align well with the essence, mission, and ends of the institution. However, boards of private, Christian colleges and universities are often self-perpetuating. The exception is church owned institutions where board members are voted on in the church's annual general meeting. But even there, the candidates are first approved by the board and often brought forward to the board development committee and board by the president.

As the board goes, so goes the institution. The board hires the president, crafts the overarching policies of the institution, awards faculty promotions, and most importantly approves faculty tenure. Their stewardship over the institution is paramount, and therefore who they are and what they do determine the future of the institution. A president looking to achieve fidelity to a Wesleyan-Holiness vision for the university must have the support of the board in pursuing the vision. Most boards look for business acumen in recruiting some members. Academic savvy is often a desirable attribute of board members. Legal competency is also often sought in some board members, and gender and ethnic balance is viewed as desirable.

At the heart of the board must be board members with theological competence and fit with a Wesleyan-Holiness vision of the university. This is especially the case if the president's strengths are in business, fund raising, or an academic field other than theology. Board members with theological competence in the Wesleyan tradition can be invaluable advisors to the board and president in ways that provide spiritual ballast to the ship and critical navigation expertise in spiritual matters. To remain effective, boards require development as well, especially in policy governance and theological wisdom. Time together budgeted for both yields significant return on the investment toward mission fulfillment.

A Strong Liberal Arts Core

An unbeatable combination in Wesleyan oriented higher education is to have a strong liberal arts core and a Wesleyan theological compass to guide how faith and the educational experience are navigated together. Among the six thousand institutions formally listed in the international index and rankings, we find extreme variance in the liberal arts core. On one end of the continuum, students may exercise complete freedom to design their educational experience, a smorgasbord approach to course selection. On the other end, the institution demands a lock-step journey through a predetermined litany of course requirements. Most Christian liberal arts institutions, including those of Wesleyan-Holiness heritage, are somewhere in the middle. A core curriculum is required with latitude in the major and elective courses if there is enough room after the core and major.

In Christian settings, three Bible courses are usually part of the core along with at least one course in philosophy, history, English literature, two in science, one or more in the social-behavioral sciences, and in some cases language competency beyond English. The core is often spread across the four years of student experience. The purpose of the core curriculum is to provide a well-rounded educational experience. With the integration of faith content, questions, and discussions, the intent is for the student to be well equipped with competencies in critical thinking, the application of learning to ethics, and the ability to communicate well in writing and speech. The aspiration of the institution is to have a powerful core curriculum that impacts all students regardless of their chosen major. This would not only include students in the humanities and sciences, but also all students in the professions (business, nursing, education). Unfortunately, what looks like a core curriculum in the liberal arts is often something less.

A core curriculum should be revamped and made over at least every ten years. A curriculum is like a well-fertilized bush. It develops sucker branches and because of them less fruit. Like the bush, it needs selective trimming and care. This is conventionally the work of the faculty under the watchful eye of the provost. The exercise is potentially a tremendous opportunity to strengthen the institution and to assure that the college or university provides a profound impact experience on every student. The exercise often fails and leaves the institution in a good state, but one that falls short of excellence, regardless of how superb each individual faculty member may be.

The reason for failure is straightforward. The process of reinventing the core too often breaks down into trade-offs between departments and programs. Every department and program is looking for strong enrollments in their courses and as many students majoring in their subject area as possible. In short, they are looking to market their major through courses required in the core, especially those in the first two years. Every department is looking for its place in the sun to market their programs and majors. The result is a core

> To move the university or college forward toward an ultimate student outcome of holiness requires the integration of head, heart, and life. Pursuing educational vitality through the integration of the academic and student life areas makes the task realistic. It requires pragmatic, integrated leadership, clear institutional priorities and direction, a strong core curriculum in the liberal arts, and program policies that promote the whole institution for the whole person, including spiritual related student outcomes.

curriculum that is too big and loaded with too many courses. When this happens, the core by default serves to introduce undecided students to their major field of study and fails to serve the greater mission of the institution.

A large, unwieldy core curriculum makes it difficult to promote an intensive experience integrating faith and learning. This is the core of the problem (no pun intended). A smaller core curriculum, especially with strong content in the humanities (English, philosophy, Bible and theology, social-behavioral studies), when well delivered by faculty committed to spiritual student outcomes, will serve the institutions vision, values, and mission. It will help to move students in the direction of the highest spiritual end, the likeness of Christ. When they are finally launched at the time of graduation, they will have momentum in the continuing development of character and core shaped competence in a way that serves them in their chosen field.

A healthy faculty will raise questions about its core curriculum along the way. Questions include: Does the core comprehensively integrate a Wesleyan understanding throughout its content over four years? Is it Christ-centered throughout? Does it help students progress along a continuum of grace? Does it promote educational vitality by being integrated with student life programs and activities?

Integrating Academic and Student Life Domains

All universities and colleges struggle with the allocation of resources between the academic program, student life (development) initiatives, and the mundane, but necessary infrastructure (preventive maintenance) needs. The conflict between academic and student life is more than a matter of budget. Academic prowess of an institution often trumps student development aspirations. In reality it is the student life area, including athletics, that continues to expand and grow faster than academics claiming more and more of the budget. This then drives the tension between the academic and student life areas. In spite of this, colleges and universities profess (market) a priority of academic excellence and academic achievement. What is lacking is a bigger vision of the student experience, one that aspires to educational vitality, one in which the academic priorities are integrated with student life aspirations. This again places priority on the whole university or college serving the whole person. The stronger, healthier model is an integrated one.

When I arrived on campus to serve as president of an excellent university, I found a high quality academic institution with a remarkable student life capacity. The problem was that the academic faculty and student life staff were at war with each other for limited resources. The former president had a passion for student life. The Academic Vice President had a passion for faculty development and superb academic departments and programs. The faculty was frustrated with not being supported like they felt they deserved. The student life leadership staff felt like they were second class citizens and underappreciated for what they achieved in student outcomes. They believed they were never officially recognized as such. The conflict was real and in some ways, toxic. If the whole university were to succeed in serving the whole person, a radical change was required. Reconciliation was the only option.

Over a period of seven years the following steps were taken to integrate the two competing arenas and meld them into one:

1. The vice president for student life position was terminated. A program-oriented provost position was established. The provost was responsible for all programs, academic and student life.

2. A strategic direction (not strategic planning) document was completed through engagement of the entire institution. This placed a priority on educational vitality (not just academic achievement). It promoted the whole university for the whole person and the

integration of the academic with student life. This communicated a clear direction for the institution.

3. Student life leaders were invited to attend and participate in faculty retreats each fall and in faculty staff meetings throughout the year.

4. A university senate was established (as opposed to a faculty senate) in which student life leadership and faculty were elected to the program governing body responsible for the educational vitality of program policies.

5. A review of student outcomes by the University Senate and related academic committees included student life related outcomes supporting the idea that the educational experience of students was more than just academic achievement. This included a focus on the whole person including outcomes related to spiritual formation and spiritual maturity.

To move the university or college forward toward an ultimate student outcome of holiness requires the integration of head, heart, and life. Pursuing educational vitality through the integration of the academic and student life areas makes the task realistic. It requires pragmatic, integrated leadership, clear institutional priorities and direction, a strong core curriculum in the liberal arts, and program policies that promote the whole institution for the whole person, including spiritual related student outcomes.

Community Covenant

A final, serious essential is the articulation of a formal covenant between the university community and each individual member including all students, faculty, staff, and boards. Such a community-wide agreement establishes the parameters of community life in support of the institution's identity in Christ and its ministry and mission. It is foundational to the idea that the whole university, in the entirety of all community members, is actively seeking positive outcomes for the whole person and for each and every person. The community covenant is best established by the participation of the whole community in discussion and dialogue about how to live with each other. It is grounded in scripture and proscribes the principles and values that all community members agree to live by and includes boundaries for interpersonal behavior supportive of life together. In short, the community covenant frames the forms within which educational vitality and personal and social holiness will be pursued.

CHAPTER THIRTEEN

THE HIGHEST SPIRITUAL ENDS

Blessed are the pure in heart for they shall see God.
Matthew 5:8

Aim at . . . a holy life.
Hebrews 12:14

The theology of John Wesley occasions clarity of classic Christian orthodoxy. In the pursuit of the highest spiritual ends, we engage a Wesleyan perspective. In the words of Frederick Coutts, "The experience of Christian holiness may be defined as one in which the whole person is redirected towards the highest spiritual end—that is, likeness to Christ, and in this he is granted the continual help of the Holy Spirit."

Spiritual Student Outcomes

From a Wesleyan-Holiness perspective, spiritual student outcomes include progress along Wesley's *via salutis* (way of salvation), his continuum of grace. From this perspective, there is something for everyone and there is always more. For the student who has not come to faith, there is the prevenient grace of God that begins the acquaintance process. For the student who has come to know Christ and experienced the justifying grace of God in Christ, there is more. There is learning to live in obedience practicing the means of grace and continuing the journey of faith in and with Christ growing in grace and Christ likeness.

This is the maturing nature of holiness with its exposures to the various means by which the student maintains proximity and has daily contact with Christ through the Holy Spirit. In the process there is an emergent intimacy that begins and matures until in yet another act of faith the student responds to the opportunity to seek God's heart cleansing crisis experience of sanctifying grace. Here holiness as process leading to spiritual maturity and holiness as crisis leading to purity of heart come together in a full salvation to the uttermost of Christ-likeness. Then the process of growing in grace and deeper maturity continues with the spiritual outcome of glorifying grace.

For the student who is new in his or her salvation, there is a salvation by grace through faith given by God saving him/her from the guilt and penalty of sin. For the student who is in the process of maturing and growing in daily grace, there is another salvation outcome. It is grace of crisis given by God saving him/her to a freedom from and power over sin. For every student, there is salvific outcomes by God's grace and the prospect of there always being more, more grace, more progress, more hope, more opportunity to become more and more like Christ until their life is radiant with God's glorifying grace.

In the ecology of holiness that characterizes a purposeful university or college, spiritual student outcomes may be achieved when the whole institution is truly committed to the development of the whole person in a holistic, integrated way. There can be a salvation student outcome for every student from the penitent student seeking salvation from sin to the student seeking purity of heart, sanctification. Upon graduation, they can be launched into life with the understanding that there is always more grace along the way in the life ahead of them. This is what we mean by "the optimism of grace." With optimism, we aspire that all students upon graduation and/or subsequently will experience the ultimate outcome of holiness, that they "be filled to the fullness of God" (Ephesians 3:19). We desire that then God may do amazing things in them and through them in service for the glory of God and the advancement of God's Kingdom (Ephesians 3:20 & 21).

Ultimate Student Outcomes

In a former appointment as president, we used a simple three word, bumper-sticker-like innovation: *Education, Transformation, Impact.* We put the three words on stationery, business cards, university literature, t-shirts, and other media that we could think of. The university was highly successful in living out the tag line. It offered quality education as documented in national surveys of universities. Its integration of the academic and student life area promoted an even higher degree of transformation including spiritual maturity. Its alumni can today be found in the various market places of life exerting Christian leadership and influence and without question having a profound impact. Is it possible that the education, transformation, and impact of that university could be even greater? The Apostle Paul's letter to the Ephesians suggests the answer to the question is yes.

In Ephesians 3:16-19, Paul prays that believers would be strengthened with power through the Holy Spirit in their inner being and that Christ may dwell in their hearts through faith. This is an outcome we aspire to see in our students. The power, capacity, understanding that Paul has in mind is the power of God's love. Paul continues by saying, "And I pray that you being rooted and established in love, may have the power with all the saints (read the whole institution for the whole person) to know this love." While that sounds cognitive and an exercise of the intellect, Paul means more: "To know this love that surpasses knowledge."

Paul is talking about the kind of learning that engages the head and the heart together, an integrated blending of the cognitive and the affective. He is referring to a comprehensive love so huge (wide, long, high, and deep) that it takes the head and the heart to grasp (not just touch) and to hold onto it in all its transforming power. If one can grasp such love that surpasses mere knowledge, then a person may be filled to all the fullness of God, the Christ dwelling, God-infilling holiness. Such education with this ultimate outcome is possible for students in a university and college that is infused with the essence of Christ, holy love. Such infusion is found in the lives of the faculty and staff who love their students so completely that they aspire to influence in every conceivable way the ultimate student outcome, life in and likeness of Christ.

Finally, it does not end there. Holiness is not an outcome for our personal enjoyment and benefit. It is a dynamic, interactive, relational state in which we are called to be servants with Christ and serve him and others. Holiness is conditioning to labor in love alongside Christ in a world that desperately needs salvation, redemption, reconciliation, and restoration. Paul's passage in Ephesians does not end with verse nineteen and the fullness of God in us. He goes on to say, "Now," now that you have the fullness of God get this right, God "is able (now) to do immeasurably more than all we ask or imagine, according to his power that is at work within us."

The immeasurably more is in and for us personally, but it is also immeasurably more in and for the world. The love that surpasses knowledge is not to be hoarded. It is to be passed on and passed out to others who are desperate to know the love of God and to be saved both from sin, and the consequences of sin in the world, and to their own experience of justifying, sanctifying, and glorifying grace. In the optimism of grace, Paul ends this passage in his letter expressing the glorifying grace in his own life as an example for us when he says, "To him (God) be glory in the church and in Christ Jesus throughout all generations, forever and ever! Amen." Here Paul resonates with the Psalmist who writes, "Not to us, O Lord, not to us, but to your name be the glory, because of your love and faithfulness."

Christian universities and colleges in the Weselyan holiness tradition were established to be a force in "spreading Scriptural holiness throughout the land." They were conceived as means of grace and venues of a higher form of higher education. They were established as centers of educational vitality, of life and light that brought students to faith, grew saints, and sent them out into the world to be an impact for the advance of the Kingdom of God. They were committed not only to a doctrine of holiness that promoted spiritual maturity, but also made possible a student's prayer, "Create in me a pure heart, O God, and renew a steadfast spirit within me. Do not cast me from your presence or take your Holy Spirit from me. Restore to me the joy of your salvation and grant me a willing spirit to sustain me" (Psalm 51:10-12).

Universities and colleges of the Wesleyan-Holiness tradition can aspire to and succeed at a form of higher education that is higher than anything presently offered. They can exemplify a form of educational vitality found in the ultimate student outcome of holiness, the fullness of God found in the likeness of Christ. Students may experience Christian holiness in which our universities and colleges intentionally direct them towards the highest spiritual end—the fullness of God in the likeness of Christ. In and through the whole institution's commitment to the whole person, students may be granted the continual help of the Holy Spirit.

ENDNOTES

Chapter One

1. Richard T. Hughes and William B. Adrian, *Models for Christian Higher Education* (Grand Rapids: Eerdmans, 1997). Hughes and Adrian provide a helpful overview of contemporary Christian higher education, engaging voices from a diverse array of institutions across the denominational and theological spectrum within Protestantism.

Chapter Two

2. *The International Encyclopedia of Higher Education* (San Francisco: Jossey-Bass, Inc., 1978, Vol. 1, offers a comprehensive review of higher education across ten volumes of essays.

3. Allegedly because John Harvard died before the founding of Harvard, he bequeathed his library and a modest endowment for books prior to the existence of Harvard and he left no pictures, paintings, or other facsimiles of himself to guide the creation of the statue that now graces Harvard yard. The motto on the statue of John Harvard was not the founding motto *(Pro Christo et Ecclesia)*. In the context of the university motto, *Veritas* (Truth), on the base of the statue, the idea that John Harvard was the Founder and

Veritas the founding motto, the whole presentation of founder and motto seems anything but *veritas*.

4. Thomas S. Kidd, *The Great Awakening: Roots of Evangelical Christianity in Colonial America* (2009). The author argues that the first Great Awakening resulted in a new form of Protestantism: evangelicalism. He defines evangelicalism in part by its attention to the Holy Spirit, particularly in revival. While others often characterize the Great Awakening groups as "Old Light" and "New Lights", the author takes the position that there were anti-revivalists, moderate evangelicals, and radical evangelicals.

Chapter Three

5. George M. Marsden, "The Soul of the American University," *First Things*, January, 1991. George Marsden's critique of Christian higher education and its demise is worth reading and discussing today. The forces and factors he presents are still present, powerful, and engaged in pulling Christian colleges and university away from first things and promoting the drift into secularism.

6. James Tunstead Burtchaell, "The Decline and Fall of the Christian College," *First Things*, May 1991. In the first of two back-to-back essays, the author presents the case study of Vanderbilt University and its disengagement from Methodism.

7. James Tunstead Burtchaell. "The Decline and Fall of the Christian College II," *First Things*, June 1991. In this second essay, the author widens the lens of his camera to look at the bigger picture of Christian higher education and its subsequent demise over time. Both essays complement the Marsden paper published by the same journal in the same year. All three have value in the quest for renewal of Christian higher education today.

Chapter Four

8. www.cccu.org. For over forty years, the Council of Christian Colleges and Universities grew into a high capacity network of evangelical institutions.

ENDNOTES

Its members together became the fastest growing segment of higher education in the United States and consistently rose in the national and regional rankings of colleges and universities. They now maintain a prominent profile among institutions across the country.

Chapter Six

9. John Wesley, *A Plain Account of Christian Perfection* (Kansas City: Beacon Hill Press, 1966. Reprinted from the complete original text as authorized by the Wesleyan conference office in London, England, in 1872.) This classic work presents the John Wesley's theological treatise on holiness.

10. Henry Knight, *The Presence of God in the Christian Life: John Wesley and the Means of Grace* (London: The Scarecrow Press, Inc., 1992). Henry Knight gives comprehensive insight into John Wesley's use of the phrase "means of grace" grounded in his theology of God's presence and identity as foundational to faith and to the end of the Christian life, a heart perfected in love.

11. Personal communication by a colleague university president at a meeting of the Association of Canadian Colleges and Universities, Spring 2008.

Chapter Seven

12. Kevin W. Mannoia, "Introduction," in Kevin W. Mannoia and Don Thorsen (eds.), *The Holiness Manifesto* (Eerdmans Publishing Co., 2008). This is a compilation of some of the papers given at the Wesleyan-holiness Study Group meetings on topics ranging from holiness in the Bible, holiness in historical and theological perspective, holiness in ministry, and holiness in the twenty-first century.

13. By the end of the three years of meetings of the Wesleyan-Holiness Study Group, its membership grew in representation from eight original denominations to thirteen. It was the beginning of what today is known as the Wesleyan-Holiness Consortium. See the WHC website: www.holinessandunity.org

14. Kenneth J. Collins, *The Theology of John Wesley: Holy Love and the Shape of Grace* (Nashville: Abingdon), 2007, 11-16. Collins presents John Wesley's theology of holy love emphasizing the role of God's prevenient, convincing grace, along with his co-operant, regenerating, sanctifying, and glorifying grace. Collins provides a window on Wesley's practical theology as a resource for discipleship and service. His work can serve well as a resource for faculty and staff who pursue a deeper understanding of Wesley's orientation to holiness.

15. A detailed history of the evolution of the WHC may be found on its website: www.holinessandunity.org

16. The complete statement of the mission, values, and goals of Aldersgate Press may be found at: www.holinessandunity.org/index.php/media/aldersgate-press/mission-vision-goals. Aldersgate Press is devoted to writing that is accessible to a broad audience interested in a deeper appreciation of contemporary Wesleyan thought regarding holiness.

Chapter Nine

17. Philip Cairns, "Foundational Discipleship, Education and Training," *Word & Deed*, Vol. 9, No. 1, November 2006. I am indebted to Phil Cairns for introducing me to the idea of form and essence originally through his paper on Salvation Army ecclesiology given at The Salvation Army's International Symposium on Theology and Ethics, Johannesburg, South Africa in August 2006. I borrow liberally from his thinking about form and essence of the church.

18. Two examples: the abandonment of slavery in England (1840) and laws against child labor (1890). William Wilberforce struggled and fought for a change in the law regarding slavery in the United Kingdom. Finally, in 1807 the British Parliament passed the Slave Trade Act abolishing slavery. Wilberforce was a committed Christian and a close friend of John Wesley who was a mentor to Wilberforce. Just prior to his death, Wesley was visited by Wilberforce. The visit gave Wesley the opportunity to encourage Wilberforce in his campaign against slavery. The perseverance of Wilberforce was a matter of a consecrated heart and a work of social

ENDNOTES

holiness. Regarding the child prostitution and sexual human trafficking, The Salvation Army in 1884 and 1885 aggressively worked to expose the weakness of existing laws that made possible child prostitution and sexual trafficking of children. Their perseverance of heart and the highly visible advocacy directly occasioned change in the law. As the law was strengthened to protect children, Salvationists view this as an impact of social holiness on society and the culture.

Chapter 10

19. Frederick Coutts, *The Call To Holiness*, (St. Albans, UK: The Campfield Press), 1957, p. 15. Coutts, the eighth international leader of The Salvation Army, writes eloquently concerning holiness with a focus on the example of Jesus and characterizes holiness in light of the fruit of the Spirit. His overarching idea of the experience of holiness is of the whole man being "redirected towards the highest spiritual end—that is the likeness to Christ."

www.ingramcontent.com/pod-product-compliance
Lightning Source LLC
Chambersburg PA
CBHW030327080526
44584CB00012B/744